SOUS VIDE COOKBOOK

Effortless Recipes for Beginners, Delicious Restaurant-Quality Meals to Make at Home, Your Perfect Go-To Guide for Every Dish Under Pressure

by **IVOR FRANKLIN**

Disclaimer:

The recipes and techniques presented in this cookbook are intended for informational purposes only. While every effort has been made to ensure the accuracy and completeness of the information provided, the author and publisher assume no responsibility for any errors or omissions, or any consequences resulting from the use of the information herein.

The recipes contained in this book may require specialized equipment and ingredients, and it is the responsibility of the reader to exercise caution and discretion when preparing and consuming these dishes. Additionally, individual dietary needs and preferences may vary, and readers are advised to consult with a qualified healthcare professional or nutritionist regarding their specific dietary requirements.

The author and publisher disclaim any liability arising directly or indirectly from the use of the recipes and techniques described in this book. By using this cookbook, readers acknowledge and agree to assume full responsibility for their actions and decisions.

Do you lead a healthy lifestyle and are looking for healthy dishes? Or do you want to learn more about new cooking technologies? Or maybe you just love delicious food? In any case, this book is for you! I invite you to the wonderful world of sous vide cooking with my Sous Vide cookbook. You will find that this amazing technology allows even beginners to cook delicious meals.

Haute cuisine today is not only about Michelin stars or the names of famous chefs. This is the alchemy of taste, born thanks to unique technologies such as sous vide. A juicy steak or aromatic seafish with al dente vegetables will be an excellent option for a family dinner. At the same time, products prepared using the sous vide technology retain their beneficial properties and supply of vitamins as much as possible.

Sous vide is a professional vacuum cooking technology that has migrated to home kitchens. Products are cooked in a water bath at a low, strictly controlled temperature.

But how can you reproduce all the necessary conditions in your own kitchen if you can't buy household appliances? First, you need to place your food in a heat-resistant zip-lock bag. Then pour water into a thick-bottomed pan and place the bag so that its neck is above the water. The pseudo-vacuum is ready. All that remains is to control the temperature using a culinary thermometer.

Unlock the secrets of fine dining in the comfort of your own kitchen with easy-to-follow recipes for beginners. This cookbook is perfect for those new to the world of sous vide cooking. She offers a variety of easy-to-follow recipes that promise to take your cooking skills to new heights.

Any meat, be it beef, veal, lamb, or pork after heat treatment in this way becomes incredibly tender, juicy, aromatic, and incredibly tasty. Vegetables, on the other hand, retain a fresh, crunchy texture that is nearly impossible with conventional cooking. You can also cook fish, seafood, poultry, and eggs using sous vide technology. You can cook anything, including desserts and soups. But the signature dish of sous vide is meat: it turns out tender and juicy. It is impossible to achieve such a result in any other way.

Cooking sous vide takes up to several hours. However, the process itself is extremely simple and does not require supervision.

Sous vide is suitable for everyone, but it will be especially appreciated by lovers of culinary experiments and anyone who cares about health and wants to eat healthy and tasty.

From juicy steaks to perfectly poached eggs and decadent desserts, my Sous Vide Cookbook is your ticket to recreating restaurant-quality meals in your home kitchen. With clear step-by-step instructions and helpful tips and tricks, you'll learn to master the art of sous vide like a seasoned pro. Each recipe describes the cooking process in as much detail as possible. With this book, you will not be left without support in the kitchen.

Whether you're hosting a dinner party or just craving a gourmet meal, this cookbook has a variety of recipes for every occasion. Having prepared even a familiar dish using the recipes from this book, you will be surprised at its depth and purity of taste. Say goodbye to guesswork and hello to culinary confidence as you discover the joy of sous vide.

Table of Contents

Introduction: 10

    Welcome to the World of Sous Vide 10

    Brief History of Sous Vide Cooking... 10

    How does it work? 11

    Benefits of Sous Vide Cooking... 11

    Essential Tips for Success 12

Chapter 2 Breakfast Recipes... 13

    Sous Vide Eggs Benedict 13

    Sous Vide French Toast: 13

    Sous Vide Breakfast Burritos:.. 14

    Sous Vide Breakfast Sausage:.. 15

    Sous Vide Yogurt: 15

    Sous Vide Oatmeal:... 16

    Sous Vide Breakfast Hash:... 17

    Sous Vide Breakfast Quiche:.. 17

    Sous Vide Bacon:... 18

    Sous Vide Breakfast Sandwiches:.. 18

    Sous Vide Quiche Lorraine 19

    Sous Vide Breakfast Casserole 20

    Sous Vide Breakfast Strata 21

    Sous Vide Cheddar and Chive Omelette 21

    Sous Vide Spinach and Feta Frittata... 22

Chapter 3 Appetizers and small snacks 24

    Sous Vide Meatballs.. 24

    Sous Vide Deviled Eggs... 24

    Sous Vide Bruschetta.. 25

    Sous Vide Stuffed Mushrooms 26

    Sous Vide Buffalo Chicken Dip.. 27

    Sous Vide Brie with Cranberry Sauce 27

    Sous Vide Sweet Potato Bites.. 28

    Sous Vide Teriyaki Meat Skewers 29

Sous Vide Lemon-Herb Salmon Bites..30

Sous Vide Chicken Satay Skewers...30

Sous Vide Bacon-Wrapped Dates..31

Sous Vide Crab Cakes 32

Sous Vide Prosciutto-Wrapped Asparagus...33

Sous Vide Spinach and Artichoke Dip Stuffed Peppers 33

Sous Vide Shrimp Cocktail...34

Sous Vide Bacon-Wrapped Scallops..35

Chapter 4 Meat Dishes..36

   Beef Recipies 36

Sous Vide Steak 36

Sous Vide Beef Short Ribs 36

Sous Vide Beef Brisket...37

Sous Vide Beef Bourguignon...38

Sous Vide Beef Tenderloin...39

Sous Vide Beef Stew..39

Sous Vide Beef Wellington...40

Sous Vide Beef Tacos...41

Sous Vide Beef Bulgogi..42

Sous Vide Beef Stir-Fry..43

Sous Vide Beef Sausages 44

   Pork Recipes 44

Sous Vide Pork Tenderloin...44

Sous Vide Pork Chops..45

Sous Vide Pork Belly..46

Sous Vide Pulled Pork..47

Sous Vide Pork Ribs...47

Sous Vide Pork Loin...48

Sous Vide Pork Carnitas...49

Sous Vide Pork Ramen 50

Sous Vide Pork Stir-Fry..51

Sous Vide Pork Sausages 52

   Lamb and Game Meats 52

Sous Vide Lamb Chops 52

Sous Vide Lamb Shoulder 53

Sous Vide Lamb Shank 53

Sous Vide Rack of Lamb 54

Sous Vide Lamb Leg 55

Sous Vide Lamb Sausages 55

Sous Vide Venison Tenderloin 56

Sous Vide Venison Backstrap 56

Sous Vide Wild Boar Shoulder 57

Sous Vide Rabbit Confit 57

Sous Vide Moose Sirloin 58

Chapter 5 Poultry 59

Chicken 59

Sous Vide Chicken Breast 59

Sous Vide Chicken Thighs 59

Sous Vide Chicken Wings 60

Sous Vide Chicken Legs 61

Sous Vide Chicken Tenders 61

Sous Vide Chicken Curry 62

Sous Vide Chicken Teriyaki 63

Sous Vide Chicken Soup 63

Sous Vide Chicken Salad 64

Sous Vide Chicken Fajitas 65

Turkey 66

Sous Vide Turkey Breast 66

Sous Vide Turkey Legs 66

Sous Vide Turkey Thighs 67

Sous Vide Turkey Wings 67

Sous Vide Turkey Roulade 68

Sous Vide Turkey Breast Roast 69

Sous Vide Turkey Meatballs 69

Sous Vide Turkey Chili 70

Sous Vide Turkey Soup 70

Sous Vide Turkey Carnitas 71

Duck 72

Sous Vide Duck Breast with Orange Sauce 72

Sous Vide Duck Leg Tacos 72

Duck Delight Sous Vide 73

Sous Vide Duck Leg Ramen 74

Sous Vide Duck Leg Confit 75

Quail 75

Sous Vide Quail with Mushroom Risotto 75

Sous Vide Quail with Bacon 76

Sous Vide Stuffed Quail 77

Dove 78

Sous Vide Dove Poppers 78

Sous Vide Dove Stew 79

Sous Vide Dove Curry 80

Chapter 6 Seafood and fish 81

Fish 81

Sous Vide Lemon Herb Salmon 81

Sous Vide Mediterranean Salmon 81

Sous Vide Smoked Salmon 82

Sous Vide Coconut Curry Salmon 83

Sous Vide Garlic Butter Salmon 83

Sous Vide Halibut with Lemon Butter Sauce 84

Sous Vide Halibut with Capers and White Wine 84

Sous Vide Halibut with Mango Salsa 85

Sous Vide Halibut with Tomato Basil Relish 86

Sous Vide Tuna Nicoise Salad 86

Sous Vide Tuna Carpaccio 87

Sous Vide Tuna with Chimichurri Sauce 88

Sous Vide Trout with Spinach and Feta 89

Sous Vide Trout with Pesto Crust 89

Sous Vide Trout with Sesame Soy Glaze 90

Sous Vide Cod with Mediterranean Vegetables 90

Sous Vide Cod with Spinach and Tomatoes 91

Simple Sous Vide Sea Bass 92

Asian-Inspired Sous Vide Sea Bass 92

Miso-Glazed Sous Vide Sea Bass 93

Sous Vide Catfish Etouffee 94

Simple Sous Vide Catfish 95

Seafood 95

Basic Sous Vide Octopus 95

Sous Vide Octopus Paella 96

Sous Vide Octopus with Romesco Sauce 97

Sous Vide Cajun Shrimp 97

Sous Vide Shrimp Scampi 98

Sous Vide BBQ Shrimp 99

Sous Vide Coconut Lime Shrimp 99

Sous Vide Garlic and Herb Grilled Shrimp 100

Sous Vide Lobster Thermidor 100

Sous Vide Lobster Ravioli 101

Sous Vide Scallops with Brown Butter Sauce 102

Sous Vide Scallops with Champagne Sauce 102

Sous Vide Scallops with Cauliflower Puree 103

Chapter 7 Sides and Vegetables 105

Sous Vide Garlic Mashed Potatoes 105

Sous Vide Green Beans with Almonds 105

Sous Vide Honey Glazed Carrots 106

Sous Vide Asparagus with Lemon Butter 106

Sous Vide Roasted Brussels Sprouts 107

Sous Vide Creamed Spinach 107

Sous Vide Glazed Baby Carrots 108

Sous Vide Corn on the Cob with Garlic Herb Butter 108

Sous Vide Sweet Potato Mash 109

Sous Vide Roasted Root Vegetables 109

Sous Vide Herbed Rice Pilaf 110

Sous Vide Honey Balsamic Glazed Brussels Sprouts 111

Sous Vide Lemon Garlic Broccoli 111

Sous Vide Parmesan Zucchini 112

Sous Vide Butternut Squash Puree 113

Chapter 8 Sous Vide for Vegetarian and Vegan recipes 114

Sous Vide Ratatouille 114

Sous Vide Cauliflower Steaks with Chimichurri Sauce 114

Sous Vide Eggplant Parmesan 115

Sous Vide Stuffed Bell Peppers with Quinoa and Vegetables 116

Sous Vide Portobello Mushrooms with Balsamic Glaze 117

Sous Vide Sweet Potato Hash 117

Sous Vide Carrot Ginger Soup 118

Sous Vide Vegan Risotto with Mushrooms 118

Sous Vide Tofu Scramble 119

Sous Vide Vegetable Curry 120

Sous Vide Butternut Squash Risotto 120

Sous Vide Beetroot Salad with Goat Cheese and Walnuts 121

Sous Vide Brussels Sprouts with Maple Glaze 122

Sous Vide Garlic Rosemary Potatoes 122

Sous Vide Coconut Curry Lentils 123

Chapter 9 Desserts 124

Sous Vide Crème Brûlée 124

Sous Vide Cheesecake 124

Sous Vide Chocolate Lava Cake 125

Sous Vide Poached Pears 126

Sous Vide Bread Pudding 126

Sous Vide Fruit Compote 127

Sous Vide Lemon Curd 127

Sous Vide Flan 128

Sous Vide Chocolate Mousse 129

Sous Vide Tiramisu 129

Conclusion 131

Introduction:

Welcome to the World of Sous Vide

Sous vide is a method of cooking food under vacuum at low temperatures. This technology is recognized as the most gentle, even ahead of steam cooking. Products prepared in sous vide, retain their beneficial properties, tastes, and aromas to the maximum extent possible. Sous vide technology has been used for 50 years in the restaurant business, and for the last 10 years - for home cooking. This is a truly proven method that has proven itself in professional kitchens.

Brief History of Sous Vide Cooking

Sous vide, which translates to "under vacuum" in French, originated in the 1970s in France.

The technique was initially developed as a method for safely and efficiently preserving food in vacuum-sealed bags by Georges Pralus, a French chef. He cooked foie gras, so sous vide is considered a gourmet method. Today it is quite affordable and has several advantages.

Sous vide cooking gained popularity in the culinary world when French chef Bruno Goussault further refined and popularized the technique in the 1970s and 1980s.

Goussault's research focused on determining precise cooking temperatures and times to achieve optimal results while maintaining the quality and integrity of the food.

In the 1990s, sous vide cooking started to gain traction in high-end restaurants in Europe and later spread to other parts of the world.

Chefs appreciated the precise control over temperature and consistency that sous vide offered, allowing them to produce consistently high-quality dishes.

Over the past couple of decades, sous vide cooking has become more accessible to home cooks with the availability of affordable sous vide machines and accessories.

Cooking enthusiasts and professionals alike have embraced sous vide for its ability to produce tender, flavorful, and evenly cooked dishes with minimal effort.

Sous vide cooking has become a staple technique in many kitchens, from Michelin-starred restaurants to home kitchens.

The popularity of sous vide continues to grow as more people discover its benefits, including convenience, precision, and the ability to achieve restaurant-quality results at home.

Chapter 1 Sous Vide Cooking

How does it work?

At first glance, it may seem that this is something extremely complicated. However, the essence of the technology is quite simple. The product is packed in a vacuum bag using a vacuum packaging machine. A package with a dish is lowered into the water of a certain temperature and subjected to languishing for a long time. Usually, the temperature is 125 - 176 °F. This can be done both in a special pan and a slow cooker or sous vide device. Such kitchen equipment is very popular because cooking in this way has many advantages. Here's how it works:

1. Preparation: The food, often meat, fish, vegetables, or even desserts, is placed in a vacuum-sealed bag along with seasonings, marinades, or sauces.

2. Sealing: The bag is vacuum-sealed to remove any air, ensuring that the food is in direct contact with the cooking liquid and preventing it from floating.

3. Water Bath: A sous vide precision cooker, also known as an immersion circulator, is attached to a pot or container filled with water. The precision cooker heats and circulates the water to maintain a constant temperature.

4. Temperature Control: The desired cooking temperature is set on the sous vide precision cooker. Unlike traditional cooking methods where the heat is transferred from the outside of the food, sous vide cooking ensures that the food is cooked evenly from edge to edge, as it is surrounded by water at a consistent temperature.

5. Cooking: The vacuum-sealed bags containing the food are submerged in the preheated water bath. The food cooks slowly and gently at the precise temperature, allowing proteins to coagulate evenly and ensuring that the food retains its moisture and flavor.

6. Finishing: After the food has cooked for the specified time, it is removed from the water bath. Depending on the recipe, the food may be finished by searing, grilling, or broiling to achieve caramelization and texture on the surface.

Sous vide cooking offers several advantages, including precise temperature control, consistent results, and enhanced flavors and textures. It is particularly popular among chefs and home cooks for cooking proteins to the perfect doneness while retaining moisture and tenderness.

Benefits of Sous Vide Cooking

With the help of this technique, you can achieve a result that is not available when using any of the common cooking methods. Judge for yourself - here are the main advantages of sous vide:

1. A completely predictable result. You don't have to worry about the product becoming hard, burning, or otherwise spoiling. Sous-vide feature – precise control of time and temperature.

2. Great texture of the finished food. You can't confuse sous-vide meat with anything - it turns out so juicy and tender. This is because the low cooking temperature delicately affects the texture.

3. No losses during heat treatment. A pan-fried steak will shrink by at least a third, and it will lose a lot of juice. Steak sous vide, on the contrary, remains juicy and retains its original volume.

4. Maximum retained benefit. Without the harmful effects of extremely high temperatures, as happens, for example, during frying, products in their finished form retain a large amount of useful substances. If we take into account that additional fat is not used in sous vide, we will get an ideal diet. But at the same time, it is delicious at the gourmet level.

5. The taste is one of the main advantages of the method. The products languish in their juice, so the dishes turn out to be aromatic, dense in texture, and delicate in taste. Loss reduction.

6. After cooking, the dish can be stored in vacuum packaging or even frozen in its finished form.

7. Sous vide dishes are suitable for those who follow the principles of healthy eating and do not want to consume extra calories. The absence of fats and carcinogens, which are formed during frying or baking, is another significant advantage.

8. No need to constantly monitor the process. It is ideal if you have a special device - you only need to set the temperature and time, and in a few hours you will get a restaurant dish for dinner. This saving of effort in the kitchen with an excellent result is a good idea for a professional kitchen as well. You don't need to constantly monitor the cooking process, and as a result, an exquisite, healthy, and tasty meal will be ready.

Essential Tips for Success

1. Use High-Quality Vacuum-Sealed Bags: Ensure that you use high-quality vacuum-sealed bags that are specifically designed for sous vide cooking. Make sure they are BPA-free and can withstand high temperatures without leaching chemicals into your food.

2. Remove Air from Bags: Properly remove air from the bags before sealing to ensure good contact between the food and the water, preventing floating during cooking.

3. Season Food Before Vacuum Sealing: Season your food with herbs, spices, marinades, or sauces before vacuum-sealing to infuse flavor into the food as it cooks.

4. Preheat Water Bath: Always preheat the water bath to the desired cooking temperature before adding the food. This ensures precise temperature control and even cooking.

5. Use a Lid or Cover: Use a lid or cover on your water bath to minimize water evaporation, maintain a consistent temperature, and reduce energy consumption.

6. Ensure Proper Water Circulation: Make sure there is enough space around the sous vide precision cooker for proper water circulation. Avoid overcrowding the water bath, which can hinder circulation and result in uneven cooking.

7. Monitor Cooking Time and Temperature: Follow recipe instructions carefully, monitoring both the cooking time and temperature to achieve the desired results. Use a reliable thermometer to ensure accuracy.

8. Sear or Finish Food After Cooking: While sous vide cooking produces perfectly cooked food, it may lack the desirable Maillard reaction for browning. Finish your food by searing, grilling, or broiling it for a delicious caramelized exterior.

9. Experiment with Cooking Times and Temperatures: Sous vide cooking allows for precise control over cooking times and temperatures. Experiment with different combinations to find the perfect balance for your preferences.

10. Practice Food Safety: Follow proper food safety guidelines, including storing and handling food properly, to minimize the risk of foodborne illness.

By following these essential tips, you can achieve consistent and delicious results with sous vide cooking, unlocking the full potential of this versatile culinary technique.

Chapter 2 Breakfast Recipes

Sous Vide Eggs Benedict

Yield: 2 servings | Prep Time: 10 minutes | Cook Time: 1 hour
Ingredients:

- 4 large eggs
- Salt and pepper to taste
- 2 English muffins, split and toasted
- 4 slices Canadian bacon or ham
- Fresh chives, chopped (optional, for garnish)

For the Hollandaise Sauce:

- 2 large egg yolks
- 1 tablespoon lemon juice
- 1/2 cup unsalted butter, melted
- Salt and pepper to taste
- Pinch of cayenne pepper (optional)

Directions:

1. Preheat Sous Vide: Fill a large pot or container with water and attach your sous vide precision cooker. Set the temperature to 145°F (63°C).
2. Prepare Eggs: Crack the eggs into individual small bowls or cups. Gently lower the eggs into the preheated water bath and cook for 1 hour.
3. Make Hollandaise Sauce: While the eggs are cooking, prepare the hollandaise sauce. In a blender or food processor, combine the egg yolks and lemon juice. Blend until frothy. With the blender running, slowly pour in the melted butter until the sauce is thick and creamy. Season with salt, pepper, and cayenne pepper if using. Keep warm until ready to use.
4. Assemble Benedict: When the eggs are almost done, toast the English muffins and heat the Canadian bacon or ham in a skillet until warmed through.
5. Plate: Remove the eggs from the water bath and carefully crack them into a bowl, being careful not to break the yolks. Season with salt and pepper.
6. Assembly: Place the toasted English muffins on plates, followed by the Canadian bacon or ham. Carefully place a sous vide egg on top of each muffin half. Spoon hollandaise sauce generously over each egg. Garnish with chopped chives if desired.

Nutritional Information: 584 calories, 27g protein, 22g carbohydrates, 44g fat, 1g fiber, 489mg cholesterol, 900mg sodium, 324mg potassium

Sous Vide French Toast:

Yield: 4 servings | Prep Time: 10 minutes | Cook Time: 1 hour
Ingredients:

- 8 slices of bread (preferably day-old)
- 4 large eggs
- 1 cup milk
- 1 teaspoon vanilla extract
- 1/2 teaspoon ground cinnamon
- 1/4 teaspoon ground nutmeg
- Pinch of salt
- Butter or cooking spray, for greasing

Directions:

1. Preheat Sous Vide: Fill a large pot or container with water and attach your sous vide precision cooker. Set the temperature to 145°F (63°C).
2. Prepare Custard Mixture: In a mixing bowl, whisk together eggs, milk, vanilla extract, cinnamon, nutmeg, and salt until well combined.
3. Dip Bread Slices: Dip each slice of bread into the custard mixture, ensuring both sides are evenly coated.
4. Vacuum Seal: Place the custard-coated bread slices in a single layer in vacuum-seal bags. Seal the bags, ensuring they are airtight.
5. Sous Vide Cooking: Submerge the sealed bags in the preheated water bath and cook for 1 hour.
6. Finish Cooking: After 1 hour, remove the bags from the water bath and carefully remove the French toast slices.
7. Sear: Heat a skillet over medium heat and melt some butter or spray with cooking spray. Sear the sous vide French toast slices for 1-2 minutes on each side until golden brown and crispy.

Nutritional Information: 310 calories, 13g protein, 37g carbohydrates, 12g fat, 2g fiber, 276mg cholesterol, 458mg sodium, 179mg potassium

Sous Vide Breakfast Burritos:

Yield: 4 servings | Prep Time: 15 minutes | Cook Time: 1 hour

Ingredients:

- 4 large eggs
- Salt and pepper to taste
- 1/2 cup diced bell peppers
- 1/2 cup diced onions
- 1/2 cup diced cooked breakfast meat (e.g., sausage, bacon, ham)
- 1/2 cup shredded cheese
- 4 large flour tortillas
- Optional toppings: salsa, avocado, sour cream

Directions:

1. Preheat Sous Vide: Fill a large pot or container with water and attach your sous vide precision cooker. Set the temperature to 167°F (75°C).
2. Prepare Eggs: Crack the eggs into individual small bowls or cups. Season with salt and pepper, then whisk until well combined. Stir in diced bell peppers, onions, and cooked breakfast meat.
3. Vacuum Seal: Divide the egg mixture evenly among the tortillas. Sprinkle shredded cheese on top. Roll up each tortilla tightly, ensuring the filling is securely enclosed. Wrap each burrito tightly in plastic wrap.
4. Sous Vide Cooking: Submerge the wrapped burritos in the preheated water bath and cook for 1 hour.
5. Finish Cooking: After 1 hour, remove the burritos from the water bath and carefully unwrap them.

6. Serve: Serve the sous vide breakfast burritos with optional toppings such as salsa, avocado, or sour cream.

Nutritional Information: 375 calories, 19g protein, 24g carbohydrates, 22g fat, 2g fiber, 293mg cholesterol, 762mg sodium, 269mg

Sous Vide Breakfast Sausage:

Yield: 4 servings | Prep Time: 10 minutes | Cook Time: 1 hour

Ingredients:

- 1 lb ground pork
- 1 teaspoon salt
- 1/2 teaspoon black pepper
- 1/2 teaspoon dried sage
- 1/2 teaspoon dried thyme
- 1/4 teaspoon ground nutmeg
- 1/4 teaspoon garlic powder
- 1/4 teaspoon onion powder
- Pinch of red pepper flakes (optional)

Directions:

1. Preheat Sous Vide: Fill a large pot or container with water and attach your sous vide precision cooker. Set the temperature to 150°F (65°C).
2. Season Ground Pork: In a mixing bowl, combine the ground pork with salt, black pepper, sage, thyme, nutmeg, garlic powder, onion powder, and red pepper flakes if using. Mix until well combined.
3. Shape Patties: Divide the seasoned pork mixture into 8 equal portions. Shape each portion into a patty, ensuring they are of uniform thickness for even cooking.
4. Vacuum Seal: Place the sausage patties in a single layer in vacuum-seal bags. Seal the bags, ensuring they are airtight.
5. Sous Vide Cooking: Submerge the sealed bags in the preheated water bath and cook for 1 hour.
6. Finish Cooking: After 1 hour, remove the bags from the water bath and carefully remove the sausage patties.
7. Sear (Optional): If desired, heat a skillet over medium-high heat and sear the sous vide sausage patties for 1-2 minutes on each side until golden brown and crispy.

Nutritional Information: 245 calories, 15g protein, 0g carbohydrates, 20g fat, 0g fiber, 67mg cholesterol, 580mg sodium, 185mg potassium

Sous Vide Yogurt:

Yield: 4 servings | Prep Time: 5 minutes | Cook Time: 8 hours (inactive)

Ingredients:

- 4 cups whole milk

- 2 tablespoons plain yogurt with live active cultures

Directions:

1. Preheat Sous Vide: Fill a large pot or container with water and attach your sous vide precision cooker. Set the temperature to 110°F (43°C).
2. Mix Milk and Yogurt: In a large mixing bowl, whisk together the whole milk and plain yogurt until well combined.
3. Fill Jars: Pour the milk and yogurt mixture into clean, sterilized jars, leaving a little space at the top for expansion. Add a tablespoon of yogurt to each jar as a starter culture.
4. Seal Jars: Secure the lids on the jars tightly.
5. Sous Vide Cooking: Submerge the sealed jars in the preheated water bath and cook for 8-12 hours.
6. Chill: After cooking, remove the jars from the water bath and let them cool to room temperature. Then transfer them to the refrigerator and chill for at least 4 hours before serving.

Nutritional Information: 160 calories, 8g protein, 12g carbohydrates, 8g fat, 0g fiber, 30mg cholesterol, 125mg sodium, 330mg potassium

Sous Vide Oatmeal:

Yield: 4 servings | Prep Time: 5 minutes | Cook Time: 1 hour

Ingredients:

- 1 cup steel-cut oats
- 4 cups water
- Pinch of salt
- Optional toppings: fresh fruit, nuts, honey, maple syrup, cinnamon

Directions:

1. Preheat Sous Vide: Fill a large pot or container with water and attach your sous vide precision cooker. Set the temperature to 155°F (68°C).
2. Combine Ingredients: In a vacuum-sealable bag or sous vide-safe container, combine the steel-cut oats, water, and a pinch of salt. Seal the bag or container.
3. Sous Vide Cooking: Submerge the sealed bag or container in the preheated water bath and cook for 1 hour.
4. Serve: After cooking, carefully remove the bag or container from the water bath. Open the bag or container and stir the oatmeal.
5. Toppings: Serve the oatmeal hot with your choice of toppings such as fresh fruit, nuts, honey, maple syrup, or cinnamon.

Nutritional Information: 150 calories, 6g protein, 27g carbohydrates, 3g fat, 4g fiber, 0mg cholesterol, 5mg sodium, 105mg potassium

Sous Vide Breakfast Hash:

Yield: 4 servings | Prep Time: 15 minutes | Cook Time: 2 hours

Ingredients:

- 2 large russet potatoes, peeled and diced
- 1/2 cup diced onions
- 1/2 cup diced bell peppers
- 1/2 cup diced cooked breakfast meat (e.g., sausage, bacon, ham)
- 2 tablespoons olive oil
- Salt and pepper to taste
- Optional toppings: fried or poached eggs, shredded cheese, hot sauce

Directions:

1. Preheat Sous Vide: Fill a large pot or container with water and attach your sous vide precision cooker. Set the temperature to 185°F (85°C).
2. Prepare Ingredients: In a bowl, toss the diced potatoes, onions, bell peppers, and cooked breakfast meat with olive oil. Season with salt and pepper to taste.
3. Vacuum Seal: Place the seasoned mixture in a single layer in vacuum-seal bags. Seal the bags, ensuring they are airtight.
4. Sous Vide Cooking: Submerge the sealed bags in the preheated water bath and cook for 2 hours.
5. Finish Cooking: After 2 hours, remove the bags from the water bath and carefully open them.
6. Sear (Optional): Heat a skillet over medium-high heat. Add the sous vide breakfast hash mixture to the skillet and cook, stirring occasionally, until lightly browned and crispy.
7. Serve: Serve the breakfast hash hot with optional toppings such as fried or poached eggs, shredded cheese, and hot sauce.

Nutritional Information: 220 calories, 6g protein, 24g carbohydrates, 12g fat, 3g fiber, 10mg cholesterol, 370mg sodium, 520mg potassium

Sous Vide Breakfast Quiche:

Yield: 4 servings | Prep Time: 15 minutes | Cook Time: 1 hour

Ingredients:

- 4 large eggs
- 1/2 cup milk or heavy cream
- Salt and pepper to taste
- 1 cup shredded cheese (e.g., cheddar, Swiss, Gruyere)
- 1/2 cup diced cooked breakfast meat (e.g., bacon, sausage, ham)
- 1/2 cup diced vegetables (e.g., bell peppers, onions, spinach)
- 1 pre-made pie crust (optional)
- Cooking spray or butter, for greasing

Directions:

1. Preheat Sous Vide: Fill a large pot or container with water and attach your sous vide precision cooker. Set the temperature to 170°F (77°C).
2. Prepare Custard Mixture: In a mixing bowl, whisk together the eggs and milk or heavy cream until well combined. Season with salt and pepper to taste.
3. Assemble Quiche Filling: Stir in the shredded cheese, diced cooked breakfast meat, and diced vegetables into the custard mixture.
4. Prepare Pie Crust (Optional): If using a pre-made pie crust, line a pie dish with the crust. Alternatively, you can skip this step for a crustless quiche.
5. Fill Pie Dish: Pour the quiche filling into the prepared pie crust or directly into a greased pie dish.
6. Vacuum Seal (Optional): If desired, you can cover the pie dish with aluminum foil and then vacuum-seal it to prevent water from seeping into the quiche during sous vide cooking.
7. Sous Vide Cooking: Submerge the sealed or uncovered pie dish in the preheated water bath and cook for 1 hour.
8. Finish Cooking: After 1 hour, remove the quiche from the water bath and let it cool slightly before slicing and serving.

Nutritional Information: 320 calories, 18g protein, 18g carbohydrates, 20g fat, 1g fiber, 210mg cholesterol, 570mg sodium, 180mg potassium

Sous Vide Bacon:

Yield: 4 servings | Prep Time: 5 minutes | Cook Time: 2 hours

Ingredients:

- 8 slices of bacon

Directions:

1. Preheat Sous Vide: Fill a large pot or container with water and attach your sous vide precision cooker. Set the temperature to 147°F (64°C).
2. Arrange Bacon: Lay the bacon slices in a single layer in a vacuum-sealable bag or sous vide-safe bag.
3. Vacuum Seal: Seal the bag, ensuring it is airtight to prevent water from entering during cooking.
4. Sous Vide Cooking: Submerge the sealed bag in the preheated water bath and cook for 2 hours.
5. Finish Cooking: After 2 hours, remove the bag from the water bath and carefully open it.
6. Sear (Optional): If desired, transfer the cooked bacon to a hot skillet or griddle and sear for 1-2 minutes on each side until browned and crispy.
7. Serve: Serve the sous vide bacon hot and enjoy!

Nutritional Information: 200 calories, 6g protein, 0g carbohydrates, 18g fat, 0g fiber, 15mg cholesterol, 500mg sodium, 50mg potassium

Sous Vide Breakfast Sandwiches:

Yield: 4 servings | Prep Time: 10 minutes | Cook Time: 1 hour

Ingredients:

- 4 large eggs
- 4 slices cheese (e.g., cheddar, Swiss)
- 4 English muffins, split and toasted
- 4 slices of cooked breakfast meat (e.g., bacon, sausage, ham)
- Salt and pepper to taste
- Butter or cooking spray, for greasing

Directions:

1. Preheat Sous Vide: Fill a large pot or container with water and attach your sous vide precision cooker. Set the temperature to 145°F (63°C).
2. Prepare Eggs: Crack the eggs into individual small bowls or cups. Season with salt and pepper to taste. Gently lower the eggs into the preheated water bath and cook for 1 hour.
3. Assemble Sandwiches: When the eggs are almost done, begin assembling the sandwiches. Place a slice of cheese on the bottom half of each English muffin. Top with a slice of cooked breakfast meat.
4. Remove Eggs: After 1 hour, remove the eggs from the water bath and carefully crack them into a bowl, being careful not to break the yolks. Season with salt and pepper.
5. Cook Eggs (Optional): If desired, melt some butter or heat cooking spray in a skillet over medium heat. Cook the sous vide eggs for 1-2 minutes on each side until the whites are set but the yolks are still runny.
6. Assemble Sandwiches: Place cooked sous vide egg on top of the breakfast meat on each English muffin. Top with the remaining English muffin halves.
7. Serve: Serve the sous vide breakfast sandwiches immediately and enjoy!

Nutritional Information: 380 calories, 21g protein, 25g carbohydrates, 20g fat, 2g fiber, 385mg cholesterol, 780mg sodium, 170mg potassium

Sous Vide Quiche Lorraine

Yield: 4 servings | Prep Time: 15 minutes | Cook Time: 1 hour

Ingredients:

- 1 pre-made pie crust
- 6 slices bacon, cooked and crumbled
- 1 cup shredded Gruyere or Swiss cheese
- 4 large eggs
- 1 cup heavy cream
- Salt and pepper to taste
- Pinch of nutmeg (optional)

Directions:

1. Preheat Sous Vide: Fill a large pot or container with water and attach your sous vide precision cooker. Set the temperature to 165°F (74°C).
2. Prepare Pie Crust: Line a pie dish with the pre-made pie crust, pressing it firmly into the bottom and sides of the dish. Trim any excess crust hanging over the edges.

3. Layer Ingredients: Sprinkle the cooked and crumbled bacon evenly over the bottom of the pie crust. Top with shredded cheese.
4. Whisk Eggs and Cream: In a mixing bowl, whisk together the eggs, heavy cream, salt, pepper, and nutmeg until well combined.
5. Pour Mixture: Carefully pour the egg and cream mixture over the bacon and cheese in the pie crust, ensuring it is evenly distributed.
6. Vacuum Seal (Optional): Cover the pie dish with aluminum foil and then vacuum-seal it to prevent water from seeping into the quiche during sous vide cooking.
7. Sous Vide Cooking: Submerge the sealed or uncovered pie dish in the preheated water bath and cook for 1 hour.
8. Finish Cooking: After 1 hour, remove the quiche from the water bath and let it cool slightly before slicing and serving.

Nutritional Information: (Values per serving) Calories: 550, Protein: 19g, Carbohydrates: 22g, Fat: 43g, Fiber: 1g, Cholesterol: 320mg, Sodium: 780mg, Potassium: 220mg

Sous Vide Breakfast Casserole

Yield: 4 servings | Prep Time: 15 minutes | Cook Time: 2 hours

Ingredients:

- 4 large eggs
- 1 cup milk
- Salt and pepper to taste
- 4 slices bread, cubed
- 1 cup shredded cheese (e.g., cheddar, Gruyere)
- 1/2 cup cooked breakfast meat (e.g., bacon, sausage, ham), diced
- 1/2 cup diced vegetables (e.g., bell peppers, onions, spinach)
- Cooking spray or butter, for greasing

Directions:

1. Preheat Sous Vide: Fill a large pot or container with water and attach your sous vide precision cooker. Set the temperature to 165°F (74°C).
2. Prepare Custard Mixture: In a mixing bowl, whisk together the eggs, milk, salt, and pepper until well combined.
3. Assemble Casserole: Grease a baking dish or casserole dish with cooking spray or butter. Layer the cubed bread, shredded cheese, cooked breakfast meat, and diced vegetables in the dish.
4. Pour Custard Mixture: Pour the prepared custard mixture over the layers in the baking dish, ensuring that the bread is evenly soaked.
5. Cover and Seal (Optional): Cover the baking dish with aluminum foil or a lid. If desired, you can also seal the dish with plastic wrap or a vacuum-sealed bag to prevent water from entering during cooking.
6. Sous Vide Cooking: Submerge the covered or sealed baking dish in the preheated water bath and cook for 2 hours.
7. Finish Cooking: After 2 hours, carefully remove the baking dish from the water bath and let it cool slightly before serving.

Nutritional Information: (Values per serving) Calories: 320, Protein: 18g, Carbohydrates: 20g, Fat: 18g, Fiber: 2g, Cholesterol: 220mg, Sodium: 560mg, Potassium: 180mg

Sous Vide Breakfast Strata

Yield: 4 servings | Prep Time: 15 minutes | Cook Time: 2 hours

Ingredients:

- 4 large eggs
- 1 cup milk
- Salt and pepper to taste
- 4 slices bread, cubed
- 1 cup shredded cheese (e.g., cheddar, Swiss)
- 1/2 cup cooked breakfast meat (e.g., bacon, sausage, ham), diced
- 1/2 cup diced vegetables (e.g., bell peppers, onions, spinach)
- Cooking spray or butter, for greasing

Directions:

1. Preheat Sous Vide: Fill a large pot or container with water and attach your sous vide precision cooker. Set the temperature to 165°F (74°C).
2. Prepare Custard Mixture: In a mixing bowl, whisk together the eggs, milk, salt, and pepper until well combined.
3. Assemble Strata: Grease a baking dish or casserole dish with cooking spray or butter. Layer the cubed bread, shredded cheese, cooked breakfast meat, and diced vegetables in the dish.
4. Pour Custard Mixture: Pour the prepared custard mixture over the layers in the baking dish, ensuring that the bread is evenly soaked.
5. Cover and Seal (Optional): Cover the baking dish with aluminum foil or a lid. If desired, you can also seal the dish with plastic wrap or a vacuum-sealed bag to prevent water from entering during cooking.
6. Sous Vide Cooking: Submerge the covered or sealed baking dish in the preheated water bath and cook for 2 hours.
7. Finish Cooking: After 2 hours, carefully remove the baking dish from the water bath and let it cool slightly before serving.

Nutritional Information: (Values per serving) Calories: 350, Protein: 20g, Carbohydrates: 22g, Fat: 20g, Fiber: 2g, Cholesterol: 240mg, Sodium: 600mg, Potassium: 200mg

Sous Vide Cheddar and Chive Omelette

Yield: 2 servings | Prep Time: 10 minutes | Cook Time: 30 minutes

Ingredients:

- 4 large eggs
- 1/4 cup shredded cheddar cheese

- 2 tablespoons chopped chives
- Salt and pepper to taste
- Cooking spray or butter, for greasing

Directions:

1. Preheat Sous Vide: Fill a large pot or container with water and attach your sous vide precision cooker. Set the temperature to 167°F (75°C).
2. Prepare Eggs: In a mixing bowl, whisk together the eggs, shredded cheddar cheese, chopped chives, salt, and pepper until well combined.
3. Grease Bag: Lightly grease a sous vide bag with cooking spray or butter to prevent sticking.
4. Pour Egg Mixture: Pour the egg mixture into the greased sous vide bag, ensuring it is evenly distributed.
5. Seal Bag: Seal the sous vide bag using a vacuum sealer or the water displacement method to remove any air and create a tight seal.
6. Sous Vide Cooking: Submerge the sealed sous vide bag in the preheated water bath and cook for 30 minutes.
7. Finish Cooking: After 30 minutes, carefully remove the sous vide bag from the water bath. Open the bag and slide the omelette onto a plate. Serve hot.

Nutritional Information: (Values per serving) Calories: 180, Protein: 15g, Carbohydrates: 2g, Fat: 12g, Fiber: 0g, Cholesterol: 380mg, Sodium: 350mg, Potassium: 150mg

Sous Vide Spinach and Feta Frittata

Yield: 4 servings | Prep Time: 15 minutes | Cook Time: 1 hour

Ingredients:

- 6 large eggs
- 1 cup fresh spinach, chopped
- 1/2 cup crumbled feta cheese
- 1/4 cup diced onions
- Salt and pepper to taste
- Cooking spray or butter, for greasing

Directions:

1. Preheat Sous Vide: Fill a large pot or container with water and attach your sous vide precision cooker. Set the temperature to 172°F (78°C).
2. Prepare Eggs: In a mixing bowl, whisk together the eggs, chopped spinach, crumbled feta cheese, diced onions, salt, and pepper until well combined.
3. Grease Bag: Lightly grease a sous vide bag with cooking spray or butter to prevent sticking.
4. Pour Egg Mixture: Pour the egg mixture into the greased sous vide bag, ensuring it is evenly distributed.
5. Seal Bag: Seal the sous vide bag using a vacuum sealer or the water displacement method to remove any air and create a tight seal.
6. Sous Vide Cooking: Submerge the sealed sous vide bag in the preheated water bath and cook for 1 hour.

7. Finish Cooking: After 1 hour, carefully remove the sous vide bag from the water bath. Open the bag and slide the frittata onto a plate. Serve hot.

Nutritional Information: (Values per serving) Calories: 170, Protein: 13g, Carbohydrates: 3g, Fat: 11g, Fiber: 1g, Cholesterol: 290mg, Sodium: 360mg, Potassium: 210mg

Chapter 3 Appetizers and small snacks

Sous Vide Meatballs

Yield: 4 servings | Prep Time: 15 minutes | Cook Time: 2 hours

Ingredients:

- 1 lb ground beef
- 1/2 cup breadcrumbs
- 1/4 cup grated Parmesan cheese
- 1/4 cup milk
- 1 egg
- 2 cloves garlic, minced
- 1 teaspoon dried oregano
- 1 teaspoon dried basil
- Salt and pepper to taste
- Marinara sauce (optional, for serving)

Directions:

1. Preheat Sous Vide: Fill a large pot or container with water and attach your sous vide precision cooker. Set the temperature to 155°F (68°C).
2. Mix Ingredients: In a large mixing bowl, combine the ground beef, breadcrumbs, Parmesan cheese, milk, egg, minced garlic, dried oregano, dried basil, salt, and pepper. Mix until well combined.
3. Form Meatballs: Using your hands, roll the mixture into golf ball-sized meatballs and place them on a plate or baking sheet.
4. Vacuum Seal (Optional): Place the meatballs in a single layer in a vacuum-sealable bag. Vacuum seal the bag to remove air and ensure the meatballs are tightly packed.
5. Sous Vide Cooking: Submerge the sealed bag of meatballs in the preheated water bath and cook for 2 hours.
6. Finish Cooking: After 2 hours, remove the bag from the water bath and carefully open it. Remove the meatballs from the bag and serve them as is or with marinara sauce if desired.

Nutritional Information: (Values per serving) Calories: 350, Protein: 25g, Carbohydrates: 10g, Fat: 20g, Fiber: 1g, Cholesterol: 120mg, Sodium: 550mg, Potassium: 380mg

Sous Vide Deviled Eggs

Yield: 4 servings | Prep Time: 15 minutes | Cook Time: 1 hour

Ingredients:

- 4 large eggs
- 2 tablespoons mayonnaise
- 1 teaspoon Dijon mustard

- 1 teaspoon white vinegar
- Salt and pepper to taste
- Paprika, for garnish (optional)
- Chopped chives, for garnish (optional)

Directions:

1. Preheat Sous Vide: Fill a large pot or container with water and attach your sous vide precision cooker. Set the temperature to 165°F (74°C).
2. Prepare Eggs: Place the eggs in a single layer in a sous vide bag or a heatproof container. Make sure they are not stacked on top of each other.
3. Sous Vide Cooking: Submerge the eggs in the preheated water bath and cook for 1 hour.
4. Ice Bath: After 1 hour, remove the eggs from the water bath and immediately transfer them to an ice bath to cool for about 10 minutes.
5. Peel Eggs: Gently peel the cooled eggs and slice them in half lengthwise. Carefully remove the yolks and place them in a mixing bowl.
6. Make Filling: Mash the egg yolks with a fork until smooth. Add mayonnaise, Dijon mustard, white vinegar, salt, and pepper to taste. Mix until well combined.
7. Fill Eggs: Spoon or pipe the yolk mixture into the hollowed-out egg whites, dividing it evenly among them.
8. Garnish: Sprinkle deviled eggs with paprika and chopped chives for garnish, if desired.

Nutritional Information: (Values per serving) Calories: 100, Protein: 6g, Carbohydrates: 1g, Fat: 8g, Fiber: 0g, Cholesterol: 190mg, Sodium: 120mg, Potassium: 70mg

Sous Vide Bruschetta

Yield: 4 servings | Prep Time: 10 minutes | Cook Time: 1 hour

Ingredients:

- 4 slices of baguette, about 1/2 inch thick
- 2 large tomatoes, diced
- 2 cloves garlic, minced
- 2 tablespoons extra virgin olive oil
- 1 tablespoon balsamic vinegar
- 1/4 cup fresh basil leaves, chopped
- Salt and pepper to taste

Directions:

1. Preheat Sous Vide: Fill a large pot or container with water and attach your sous vide precision cooker. Set the temperature to 140°F (60°C).
2. Prepare Baguette: Place the slices of baguette in a single layer in a sous vide bag or a heatproof container.
3. Sous Vide Cooking: Submerge the baguette slices in the preheated water bath and cook for 1 hour.
4. Prepare Bruschetta Topping: In a mixing bowl, combine diced tomatoes, minced garlic, extra virgin olive oil, balsamic vinegar, chopped basil leaves, salt, and pepper. Mix well to combine.

5. Toast Baguette: After 1 hour, remove the baguette slices from the water bath and carefully remove them from the bag. Transfer them to a baking sheet and broil in the oven for 2-3 minutes on each side until lightly toasted.
6. Assemble Bruschetta: Once toasted, top each baguette slice with the prepared tomato mixture, dividing it evenly among them.
7. Serve: Arrange the bruschetta on a serving platter and serve immediately.

Nutritional Information: (Values per serving) Calories: 180, Protein: 3g, Carbohydrates: 20g, Fat: 10g, Fiber: 2g, Cholesterol: 0mg, Sodium: 250mg, Potassium: 200mg

Sous Vide Stuffed Mushrooms

Yield: 4 servings | Prep Time: 20 minutes | Cook Time: 1 hour

Ingredients:

- 12 large cremini or button mushrooms, stems removed and reserved
- 4 oz cream cheese, softened
- 1/4 cup grated Parmesan cheese
- 2 cloves garlic, minced
- 2 tablespoons chopped fresh parsley
- Salt and pepper to taste
- Olive oil for drizzling
- Optional: breadcrumbs for topping

Directions:

1. Preheat Sous Vide: Fill a large pot or container with water and attach your sous vide precision cooker. Set the temperature to 165°F (74°C).
2. Prepare Mushrooms: Clean the mushrooms and remove the stems. Set the mushroom caps aside and finely chop the stems.
3. Make Filling: In a mixing bowl, combine the chopped mushroom stems, softened cream cheese, grated Parmesan cheese, minced garlic, chopped parsley, salt, and pepper. Mix until well combined.
4. Fill Mushrooms: Spoon the cream cheese mixture into the mushroom caps, dividing it evenly among them.
5. Vacuum Seal (Optional): Place the stuffed mushrooms in a single layer in a vacuum-sealable bag. Vacuum seal the bag to remove air and ensure the mushrooms are tightly packed.
6. Sous Vide Cooking: Submerge the sealed bag of stuffed mushrooms in the preheated water bath and cook for 1 hour.
7. Finish Cooking: After 1 hour, carefully remove the bag from the water bath. Open the bag and remove the stuffed mushrooms.
8. Optional: Toast Breadcrumbs: If desired, preheat the oven to 375°F (190°C). Place the stuffed mushrooms on a baking sheet, drizzle with olive oil, and sprinkle with breadcrumbs. Bake for 10-15 minutes until golden brown.
9. Serve: Arrange the stuffed mushrooms on a serving platter and serve hot.

Nutritional Information: (Values per serving) Calories: 120, Protein: 5g, Carbohydrates: 4g, Fat: 9g, Fiber: 1g, Cholesterol: 25mg, Sodium: 180mg, Potassium: 300mg

Sous Vide Buffalo Chicken Dip

Yield: 4 servings | Prep Time: 15 minutes | Cook Time: 1 hour

Ingredients:

- 2 chicken breasts, boneless and skinless
- 1/2 cup buffalo sauce
- 1/2 cup cream cheese, softened
- 1/2 cup sour cream
- 1/2 cup shredded cheddar cheese
- 1/4 cup blue cheese crumbles
- 2 green onions, chopped
- Salt and pepper to taste
- Tortilla chips or celery sticks, for serving

Directions:

1. Preheat Sous Vide: Fill a large pot or container with water and attach your sous vide precision cooker. Set the temperature to 150°F (65°C).
2. Prepare Chicken: Season the chicken breasts with salt and pepper on both sides. Place them in a vacuum-sealable bag or a zip-top bag. Pour the buffalo sauce into the bag, ensuring the chicken is coated evenly. Seal the bag using the water displacement method or a vacuum sealer.
3. Sous Vide Cooking: Submerge the sealed bag of chicken breasts in the preheated water bath and cook for 1 hour.
4. Shred Chicken: After 1 hour, remove the bag from the water bath. Open the bag and transfer the cooked chicken breasts to a bowl. Use two forks to shred the chicken into bite-sized pieces.
5. Prepare Dip Mixture: In a mixing bowl, combine the shredded chicken, softened cream cheese, sour cream, shredded cheddar cheese, and blue cheese crumbles. Mix until well combined.
6. Broil (Optional): Preheat the broiler in your oven. Transfer the dip mixture to a heatproof baking dish. Place it under the broiler for 5-7 minutes until the top is bubbly and golden brown.
7. Serve: Remove the dip from the oven and sprinkle chopped green onions on top. Serve hot with tortilla chips or celery sticks for dipping.

Nutritional Information: (Values per serving) Calories: 320, Protein: 25g, Carbohydrates: 5g, Fat: 22g, Fiber: 1g, Cholesterol: 95mg, Sodium: 850mg, Potassium: 330mg

Sous Vide Brie with Cranberry Sauce

Yield: 4 servings | Prep Time: 10 minutes | Cook Time: 1 hour

Ingredients:

- 1 wheel of brie cheese (about 8 oz)
- 1/2 cup cranberry sauce
- 2 tablespoons honey
- 1 tablespoon water

- Fresh rosemary sprigs, for garnish
- Crackers or bread, for serving

Directions:

1. Preheat Sous Vide: Fill a large pot or container with water and attach your sous vide precision cooker. Set the temperature to 130°F (54°C).
2. Prepare Brie: Remove any packaging from the brie cheese and place it in a vacuum-sealable bag or a zip-top bag. Seal the bag using the water displacement method or a vacuum sealer.
3. Sous Vide Cooking: Submerge the sealed bag of brie cheese in the preheated water bath and cook for 1 hour.
4. Prepare Cranberry Sauce: In a small saucepan, combine the cranberry sauce, honey, and water. Heat over medium heat, stirring occasionally, until the sauce is warmed through and slightly thickened. Remove from heat and set aside.
5. Remove Brie: After 1 hour, remove the bag of brie cheese from the water bath and carefully open it.
6. Serve: Transfer the cooked brie to a serving plate or platter. Spoon the warm cranberry sauce over the top of the brie. Garnish with fresh rosemary sprigs. Serve the sous vide brie with cranberry sauce immediately with crackers or bread for dipping.

Nutritional Information: (Values per serving) Calories: 280, Protein: 12g, Carbohydrates: 20g, Fat: 18g, Fiber: 1g, Cholesterol: 50mg, Sodium: 300mg, Potassium: 150mg

Sous Vide Sweet Potato Bites

Yield: 4 servings | Prep Time: 15 minutes | Cook Time: 1 hour

Ingredients:

- 2 medium sweet potatoes, peeled and cut into 1-inch cubes
- 2 tablespoons olive oil
- 1 teaspoon garlic powder
- 1 teaspoon smoked paprika
- Salt and pepper to taste
- Optional: chopped fresh parsley or cilantro for garnish

Directions:

1. Preheat Sous Vide: Fill a large pot or container with water and attach your sous vide precision cooker. Set the temperature to 185°F (85°C).
2. Season Sweet Potatoes: In a mixing bowl, toss the sweet potato cubes with olive oil, garlic powder, smoked paprika, salt, and pepper until evenly coated.
3. Vacuum Seal (Optional): Place the seasoned sweet potato cubes in a single layer in a vacuum-sealable bag. Vacuum seal the bag to remove air and ensure the sweet potatoes are tightly packed.
4. Sous Vide Cooking: Submerge the sealed bag of sweet potato cubes in the preheated water bath and cook for 1 hour.
5. Finish Cooking: After 1 hour, carefully remove the bag from the water bath. Open the bag and remove the sweet potato cubes.
6. Optional: Sear (Optional): Preheat a skillet over medium-high heat. Add a bit of olive oil to the skillet and sear the sweet potato cubes for 1-2 minutes on each side until lightly browned and crispy.

7. Serve: Transfer the sous vide sweet potato bites to a serving plate or platter. Garnish with chopped fresh parsley or cilantro, if desired. Serve hot as a side dish or appetizer.

Nutritional Information: (Values per serving) Calories: 120, Protein: 2g, Carbohydrates: 18g, Fat: 5g, Fiber: 3g, Cholesterol: 0mg, Sodium: 90mg, Potassium: 320mg

Sous Vide Teriyaki Meat Skewers

Yield: 4 servings | Prep Time: 15 minutes | Cook Time: 1 hour

Ingredients:

- 1 lb boneless chicken breast or beef sirloin, cut into 1-inch cubes
- 1/2 cup teriyaki sauce
- 2 tablespoons soy sauce
- 2 tablespoons honey
- 2 cloves garlic, minced
- 1 teaspoon grated ginger
- 1 tablespoon sesame oil
- Wooden or metal skewers
- Optional garnish: sliced green onions and sesame seeds

Directions:

1. Preheat Sous Vide: Fill a large pot or container with water and attach your sous vide precision cooker. Set the temperature to 145°F (63°C) for chicken or 135°F (57°C) for beef.
2. Prepare Marinade: In a mixing bowl, whisk together the teriyaki sauce, soy sauce, honey, minced garlic, grated ginger, and sesame oil.
3. Marinate Meat: Place the cubed chicken or beef in a shallow dish or a resealable plastic bag. Pour the marinade over the meat, making sure it is evenly coated. Marinate in the refrigerator for at least 30 minutes, or overnight for best results.
4. Skewer Meat: Thread the marinated meat onto skewers, dividing it evenly among them. If using wooden skewers, soak them in water for 30 minutes beforehand to prevent burning.
5. Sous Vide Cooking: Submerge the skewers in the preheated water bath and cook for 1 hour.
6. Finish (Optional): After 1 hour, remove the skewers from the water bath. Preheat a grill or grill pan over medium-high heat. Grill the skewers for 1-2 minutes on each side to achieve a charred exterior, basting with any remaining marinade.
7. Serve: Transfer the cooked teriyaki meat skewers to a serving platter. Garnish with sliced green onions and sesame seeds, if desired. Serve hot as an appetizer or main dish, with rice or vegetables on the side.

Nutritional Information: (Values per serving) Calories: 250, Protein: 25g, Carbohydrates: 15g, Fat: 10g, Fiber: 1g,

Cholesterol: 70mg, Sodium: 800mg, Potassium: 350mg

Sous Vide Lemon-Herb Salmon Bites

Yield: 4 servings | Prep Time: 10 minutes | Cook Time: 30 minutes

Ingredients:

- 1 lb skinless salmon fillet, cut into bite-sized cubes
- 2 tablespoons olive oil
- 2 cloves garlic, minced
- Zest of 1 lemon
- 1 tablespoon lemon juice
- 1 tablespoon chopped fresh dill
- 1 tablespoon chopped fresh parsley
- Salt and pepper to taste
- Lemon wedges, for serving

Directions:

1. Preheat Sous Vide: Fill a large pot or container with water and attach your sous vide precision cooker. Set the temperature to 130°F (54°C).
2. Season Salmon: In a mixing bowl, combine the olive oil, minced garlic, lemon zest, lemon juice, chopped dill, chopped parsley, salt, and pepper. Add the salmon cubes to the bowl and toss to coat evenly.
3. Vacuum Seal (Optional): Place the seasoned salmon cubes in a single layer in a vacuum-sealable bag. Vacuum seal the bag to remove air and ensure the salmon is tightly packed.
4. Sous Vide Cooking: Submerge the sealed bag of salmon cubes in the preheated water bath and cook for 30 minutes.
5. Remove Salmon: After 30 minutes, carefully remove the bag from the water bath. Open the bag and remove the salmon cubes.
6. Serve: Transfer the sous vide lemon-herb salmon bites to a serving plate. Serve with lemon wedges on the side for squeezing over the salmon.

Nutritional Information: (Values per serving) Calories: 220, Protein: 25g, Carbohydrates: 1g, Fat: 13g, Fiber: 0g, Cholesterol: 70mg, Sodium: 80mg, Potassium: 450mg

Sous Vide Chicken Satay Skewers

Yield: 4 servings | Prep Time: 15 minutes | Cook Time: 1 hour

Ingredients:

- 1 lb boneless, skinless chicken breasts, cut into thin strips
- 1/4 cup coconut milk
- 2 tablespoons soy sauce
- 1 tablespoon fish sauce
- 1 tablespoon brown sugar
- 2 cloves garlic, minced

- 1 teaspoon ground turmeric
- 1 teaspoon ground coriander
- 1/2 teaspoon ground cumin
- 1/2 teaspoon ground ginger
- Bamboo skewers, soaked in water for 30 minutes
- Chopped peanuts and chopped cilantro, for garnish (optional)
- Peanut sauce, for dipping (optional)

Directions:

1. Preheat Sous Vide: Fill a large pot or container with water and attach your sous vide precision cooker. Set the temperature to 140°F (60°C).
2. Prepare Marinade: In a mixing bowl, combine the coconut milk, soy sauce, fish sauce, brown sugar, minced garlic, ground turmeric, ground coriander, ground cumin, and ground ginger. Mix until well combined.
3. Marinate Chicken: Place the chicken strips in a shallow dish or resealable plastic bag. Pour the marinade over the chicken, ensuring each piece is coated evenly. Marinate in the refrigerator for at least 30 minutes, or overnight for best results.
4. Skewer Chicken: Thread the marinated chicken strips onto the soaked bamboo skewers, dividing them evenly among the skewers.
5. Sous Vide Cooking: Submerge the skewers in the preheated water bath and cook for 1 hour.
6. Finish (Optional): After 1 hour, remove the skewers from the water bath. Preheat a grill or grill pan over medium-high heat. Grill the chicken skewers for 1-2 minutes on each side to achieve grill marks and caramelization.
7. Serve: Transfer the sous vide chicken satay skewers to a serving platter. Garnish with chopped peanuts and cilantro, if desired. Serve with peanut sauce for dipping, if desired.

Nutritional Information: (Values per serving) Calories: 220, Protein: 25g, Carbohydrates: 5g, Fat: 10g, Fiber: 1g, Cholesterol: 65mg, Sodium: 480mg, Potassium: 350mg

Sous Vide Bacon-Wrapped Dates

Yield: 4 servings | Prep Time: 15 minutes | Cook Time: 1 hour

Ingredients:

- 12 large Medjool dates, pitted
- 6 slices bacon, cut in half crosswise
- 1/4 cup goat cheese (optional)
- Toothpicks, for securing

Directions:

1. Preheat Sous Vide: Fill a large pot or container with water and attach your sous vide precision cooker. Set the temperature to 150°F (65°C).
2. Prepare Dates: If the dates are not already pitted, carefully slice them open and remove the pits. If desired, stuff each date with a small amount of goat cheese.

3. Wrap with Bacon: Take each pitted date and wrap it with a half-slice of bacon. Secure the bacon in place by inserting a toothpick through the center of the date.
4. Bag and Seal: Place the bacon-wrapped dates in a single layer in a resealable sous vide bag. Arrange them so they do not overlap. Seal the bag using the water displacement method or a vacuum sealer.
5. Sous Vide Cooking: Submerge the sealed bag of bacon-wrapped dates in the preheated water bath. Cook for 1 hour.
6. Finish (Optional): After 1 hour, remove the bag from the water bath and carefully remove the bacon-wrapped dates. If desired, you can finish them by searing them in a hot skillet or under a broiler for a few minutes to crisp up the bacon.
7. Serve: Transfer the sous vide bacon-wrapped dates to a serving platter and serve hot.

Nutritional Information: (Values per serving) Calories: 180, Protein: 4g, Carbohydrates: 25g, Fat: 8g, Fiber: 3g, Cholesterol: 10mg, Sodium: 200mg, Potassium: 380mg

Sous Vide Crab Cakes

Yield: 4 servings | Prep Time: 20 minutes | Cook Time: 1 hour

Ingredients:

- 1 lb lump crab meat
- 1/2 cup breadcrumbs
- 1/4 cup mayonnaise
- 1 large egg, beaten
- 2 tablespoons chopped fresh parsley
- 1 tablespoon Dijon mustard
- 1 tablespoon lemon juice
- 1 teaspoon Old Bay seasoning
- Salt and pepper to taste
- 2 tablespoons olive oil (for searing)

Directions:

1. Preheat Sous Vide: Fill a large pot or container with water and attach your sous vide precision cooker. Set the temperature to 135°F (57°C).
2. Prepare Crab Mixture: In a large mixing bowl, combine the lump crab meat, breadcrumbs, mayonnaise, beaten egg, chopped parsley, Dijon mustard, lemon juice, Old Bay seasoning, salt, and pepper. Gently mix until well combined.
3. Form Crab Cakes: Divide the crab mixture into 4 equal portions. Shape each portion into a round crab cake, about 1 inch thick. Place the crab cakes on a plate or baking sheet lined with parchment paper.
4. Bag and Seal: Place the plate of crab cakes in a single layer in a resealable sous vide bag. Seal the bag using the water displacement method or a vacuum sealer.
5. Sous Vide Cooking: Submerge the sealed bag of crab cakes in the preheated water bath. Cook for 1 hour.
6. Finish (Optional): After 1 hour, remove the bag from the water bath and carefully remove the crab cakes from the bag. If desired, you can gently sear the crab cakes in a hot skillet with olive oil for 1-2 minutes on each side to brown the exterior.

7. Serve: Transfer the sous vide crab cakes to a serving platter and serve hot, garnished with lemon wedges and additional chopped parsley if desired.

Nutritional Information: (Values per serving) Calories: 290, Protein: 24g, Carbohydrates: 9g, Fat: 17g, Fiber: 1g, Cholesterol: 155mg, Sodium: 680mg, Potassium: 320mg

Sous Vide Prosciutto-Wrapped Asparagus

Yield: 4 servings | Prep Time: 15 minutes | Cook Time: 30 minutes

Ingredients:

- 1 lb asparagus spears, tough ends trimmed
- 8 slices prosciutto
- 2 tablespoons olive oil
- Salt and black pepper, to taste
- Optional: grated Parmesan cheese, for garnish

Directions:

1. Preheat Sous Vide: Fill a large pot or container with water and attach your sous vide precision cooker. Set the temperature to 180°F (82°C).
2. Prepare Asparagus: Divide the asparagus spears into 8 equal bundles. Wrap each bundle tightly with a slice of prosciutto, covering as much of the asparagus as possible. Place the wrapped asparagus bundles in a single layer in a resealable sous vide bag.
3. Season and Seal: Drizzle the olive oil over the wrapped asparagus bundles. Season with salt and black pepper to taste. Seal the bag using the water displacement method or a vacuum sealer.
4. Sous Vide Cooking: Submerge the sealed bag of prosciutto-wrapped asparagus in the preheated water bath. Cook for 30 minutes.
5. Finish (Optional): After 30 minutes, remove the bag from the water bath and carefully remove the prosciutto-wrapped asparagus bundles. If desired, you can finish them by searing them in a hot skillet with a little olive oil for 1-2 minutes on each side to crisp up the prosciutto.
6. Serve: Transfer the sous vide prosciutto-wrapped asparagus to a serving platter. Garnish with grated Parmesan cheese if desired, and serve hot.

Nutritional Information: (Values per serving) Calories: 160, Protein: 9g, Carbohydrates: 4g, Fat: 12g, Fiber: 2g, Cholesterol: 15mg, Sodium: 600mg, Potassium: 380mg

Sous Vide Spinach and Artichoke Dip Stuffed Peppers

Yield: 4 servings | Prep Time: 15 minutes | Cook Time: 2 hours

Ingredients:

- 4 large bell peppers (any color), halved and seeded
- 1 cup frozen spinach, thawed and excess moisture squeezed out

- 1 cup canned artichoke hearts, chopped
- 1 cup shredded mozzarella cheese
- 1/2 cup grated Parmesan cheese
- 1/2 cup cream cheese, softened
- 1/4 cup mayonnaise
- 2 cloves garlic, minced
- 1 teaspoon onion powder
- Salt and pepper, to taste
- Olive oil, for drizzling
- Chopped fresh parsley, for garnish (optional)

Directions:

1. Preheat Sous Vide: Fill a large pot or container with water and attach your sous vide precision cooker. Set the temperature to 175°F (80°C).
2. Prepare Peppers: Season the inside of each bell pepper half with salt and pepper. Place them in a single layer in a large resealable sous vide bag.
3. Prepare Filling: In a mixing bowl, combine the thawed spinach, chopped artichoke hearts, mozzarella cheese, Parmesan cheese, cream cheese, mayonnaise, minced garlic, and onion powder. Mix until well combined. Season with salt and pepper to taste.
4. Stuff Peppers: Spoon the spinach and artichoke dip mixture into each bell pepper half, filling them evenly.
5. Seal Bag: Drizzle a little olive oil over the stuffed peppers. Seal the sous vide bag using the water displacement method or a vacuum sealer.
6. Sous Vide Cooking: Submerge the sealed bag of stuffed peppers in the preheated water bath. Cook for 2 hours.
7. Finish and Serve: After 2 hours, remove the bag from the water bath and carefully remove the stuffed peppers. Transfer them to a serving platter, garnish with chopped fresh parsley if desired, and serve hot.

Nutritional Information: (Values per serving) Calories: 300, Protein: 14g, Carbohydrates: 12g, Fat: 23g, Fiber: 3g, Cholesterol: 60mg, Sodium: 520mg, Potassium: 480mg

Sous Vide Shrimp Cocktail

Yield: 4 servings | Prep Time: 10 minutes | Cook Time: 30 minutes

Ingredients:

- 1 pound large shrimp, peeled and deveined
- 1 lemon, thinly sliced
- 2 cloves garlic, minced
- 1 tablespoon olive oil
- 1 teaspoon paprika
- Salt and pepper, to taste
- Cocktail sauce, for serving
- Lemon wedges, for serving
- Fresh parsley, for garnish (optional)

Directions:

1. Preheat Sous Vide: Fill a large pot or container with water and attach your sous vide precision cooker. Set the temperature to 135°F (57°C).
2. Season Shrimp: In a mixing bowl, combine the peeled and deveined shrimp with minced garlic, olive oil, paprika, salt, and pepper. Toss until the shrimp are evenly coated.
3. Vacuum Seal: Arrange the seasoned shrimp and lemon slices in a single layer in a vacuum-sealable bag or a resealable sous vide bag. Seal the bag, ensuring it is airtight.
4. Sous Vide Cooking: Submerge the sealed bag of shrimp in the preheated water bath. Cook for 30 minutes.
5. Chill Shrimp: Once cooked, remove the bag from the water bath and immediately transfer the shrimp to an ice bath to chill for a few minutes. This helps to stop the cooking process and keep the shrimp firm and juicy.
6. Serve: Drain the chilled shrimp and arrange them on a serving platter. Serve with cocktail sauce, and lemon wedges, and garnish with fresh parsley if desired.

Nutritional Information: (Values per serving) Calories: 150, Protein: 22g, Carbohydrates: 2g, Fat: 6g, Fiber: 0g, Cholesterol: 220mg, Sodium: 500mg, Potassium: 180mg

Sous Vide Bacon-Wrapped Scallops

Yield: 4 servings | Prep Time: 15 minutes | Cook Time: 1 hour

Ingredients:

- 12 large sea scallops
- 12 slices of bacon
- Salt and pepper, to taste
- Lemon wedges, for serving
- Fresh parsley, chopped, for garnish (optional)

Directions:

1. Preheat Sous Vide: Fill a large pot or container with water and attach your sous vide precision cooker. Set the temperature to 130°F (54°C).
2. Prepare Scallops: Pat the scallops dry with paper towels. Season each scallop with salt and pepper to taste.
3. Wrap with Bacon: Wrap each scallop with a slice of bacon, securing it with a toothpick if necessary.
4. Vacuum Seal: Arrange the bacon-wrapped scallops in a single layer in a vacuum-sealable bag or a resealable sous vide bag. Seal the bag, ensuring it is airtight.
5. Sous Vide Cooking: Submerge the sealed bag of scallops in the preheated water bath. Cook for 1 hour.
6. Finish: After 1 hour, remove the bag from the water bath and carefully take out the scallops.
7. Sear (Optional): If desired, you can give the scallops a quick sear in a hot skillet or on a grill to crisp up the bacon.
8. Serve: Transfer the scallops to a serving platter, garnish with chopped parsley if using, and serve with lemon wedges on the side.

Nutritional Information: (Values per serving) Calories: 290, Protein: 20g, Carbohydrates: 1g, Fat: 23g, Fiber: 0g, Cholesterol: 55mg, Sodium: 450mg, Potassium: 340mg

Chapter 4 Meat Dishes

Beef Recipies

Sous Vide Steak

Yield: 4 servings | Prep Time: 10 minutes | Cook Time: 1 hour

Ingredients:

- 4 (8-ounce) steaks (such as ribeye, sirloin, or filet mignon)
- Salt and pepper, to taste
- 2 cloves garlic, minced (optional)
- 2 sprigs fresh rosemary (optional)
- 2 tablespoons olive oil (optional)
- Butter for searing (optional)

Directions:

1. Preheat the sous vide water bath to your desired doneness temperature: 130°F (54°C) for medium-rare, 140°F (60°C) for medium, or 150°F (66°C) for medium-well.
2. Season the steaks generously with salt and pepper. Add minced garlic, fresh rosemary, and olive oil if desired for extra flavor.
3. Place each seasoned steak in a separate sous vide bag, removing any air and sealing them tightly.
4. Once the water bath reaches the desired temperature, immerse the bags containing the steaks into the water.
5. Cook the steaks for 1 hour, ensuring they are fully submerged.
6. After cooking, remove the steaks from the sous vide bags and pat them dry with paper towels.
7. Optional step: Heat a skillet over high heat and add butter. Sear the steaks for 1-2 minutes on each side until a golden crust forms.

Nutritional information: Approximately 500 calories, 50g protein, 0g carbohydrates, 32g fat, 0g fiber, 150mg cholesterol, 400mg sodium, 700mg potassium per serving.

Sous Vide Beef Short Ribs

Yield: 4 servings | Prep Time: 10 minutes | Cook Time: 24 hours

Ingredients:

- 4 beef short ribs, bone-in, about 1 pound each
- Salt and pepper, to taste
- 2 cloves garlic, minced
- 2 sprigs of fresh thyme

- 2 tablespoons olive oil
- 1 cup beef broth (optional)

Directions:

1. Preheat the sous vide water bath to 160°F (71°C).
2. Season the beef short ribs generously with salt and pepper.
3. Divide minced garlic, fresh thyme, and olive oil evenly among the short ribs, rubbing the seasonings into the meat.
4. Place each seasoned short rib in a separate sous vide bag, adding beef broth if desired for added flavor.
5. Remove any air from the bags and seal them tightly.
6. Once the water bath reaches the desired temperature, submerge the bags containing the short ribs into the water.
7. Cook the short ribs for 24 hours, ensuring they are fully submerged throughout the cooking process.
8. After cooking, remove the short ribs from the sous vide bags and pat them dry with paper towels.
9. Optional step: Preheat a grill or skillet to high heat and sear the short ribs for 1-2 minutes on each side until a caramelized crust forms.

Nutritional information: Approximately 600 calories, 50g protein, 0g carbohydrates, 45g fat, 0g fiber, 180mg cholesterol, 800mg sodium, 700mg potassium per serving.

Sous Vide Beef Brisket

Yield: 4 servings | Prep Time: 10 minutes | Cook Time: 24 hours

Ingredients:

- 2-3 pounds beef brisket
- Salt and pepper, to taste
- 2 cloves garlic, minced
- 2 tablespoons brown sugar
- 1 tablespoon paprika
- 1 teaspoon onion powder
- 1 teaspoon garlic powder
- 1/2 teaspoon cayenne pepper (optional)
- 1 cup beef broth
- 2 tablespoons olive oil

Directions:

1. Season the beef brisket generously with salt and pepper.
2. In a small bowl, mix minced garlic, brown sugar, paprika, onion powder, garlic powder, and cayenne pepper (if using).
3. Rub the spice mixture evenly over the surface of the brisket.
4. Place the seasoned brisket in a sous vide bag and add beef broth and olive oil.
5. Remove any air from the bag and seal it tightly.
6. Preheat the sous vide water bath to 155°F (68°C) and cook the brisket for 24 hours, ensuring it is fully submerged throughout the cooking process.
7. After cooking, remove the brisket from the sous vide bag and pat it dry with paper towels.

8. Optional step: Preheat a grill or skillet to high heat and sear the brisket for 1-2 minutes on each side until a caramelized crust forms.

Nutritional information: Approximately 500 calories, 45g protein, 5g carbohydrates, 30g fat, 0g fiber, 120mg cholesterol, 800mg sodium, 600mg potassium per serving.

Sous Vide Beef Bourguignon

Yield: 4 servings | Prep Time: 20 minutes | Cook Time: 24 hours

Ingredients:

- 1.5 pounds beef chuck roast, cut into chunks
- Salt and pepper, to taste
- 2 tablespoons all-purpose flour
- 2 tablespoons olive oil
- 4 slices bacon, chopped
- 1 onion, diced
- 2 carrots, diced
- 2 cloves garlic, minced
- 1 cup red wine (such as Burgundy or Pinot Noir)
- 1 cup beef broth
- 2 tablespoons tomato paste
- 2 bay leaves
- 1 teaspoon dried thyme
- 1/2 pound mushrooms, sliced
- 1/4 cup fresh parsley, chopped (for garnish)

Directions:

1. Season the beef chuck roast chunks with salt and pepper, then coat them evenly with flour.
2. In a large skillet, heat the olive oil over medium-high heat. Brown the beef chunks on all sides, working in batches if necessary. Transfer the browned beef to a plate. In the same skillet, add the chopped bacon and cook until crispy. Remove the bacon and set aside, leaving the rendered fat in the skillet. Add the diced onion and carrots to the skillet and cook until softened about 5 minutes. Add the minced garlic and cook for an additional minute.
3. Deglaze the skillet with the red wine, scraping up any browned bits from the bottom of the pan. Stir in the beef broth, tomato paste, bay leaves, and dried thyme.
4. Transfer the beef, bacon, and vegetable mixture to a sous vide bag. Seal the bag tightly, removing any air.
5. Preheat the sous vide water bath to 155°F (68°C) and cook the beef bourguignon for 24 hours.
6. About 30 minutes before serving, heat a skillet over medium heat and sauté the sliced mushrooms until golden brown and tender.
7. Remove the beef bourguignon from the sous vide bath, open the bag, and transfer the contents to a serving dish. Discard the bay leaves.
8. Garnish with sautéed mushrooms and chopped parsley before serving.

Nutritional information: Approximately 450 calories, 30g protein, 15g carbohydrates, 25g fat, 3g fiber, 85mg cholesterol, 800mg sodium, 800mg potassium per serving.

Sous Vide Beef Tenderloin

Yield: 4 servings | Prep Time: 10 minutes | Cook Time: 1 hour

Ingredients:

- 2 pounds beef tenderloin
- Salt and pepper, to taste
- 2 cloves garlic, minced
- 2 tablespoons olive oil
- 2 sprigs of fresh thyme
- 2 tablespoons butter (optional, for searing)

Directions:

1. Preheat the sous vide water bath to 130°F (54°C) for medium-rare, 140°F (60°C) for medium, or 150°F (66°C) for medium-well.
2. Season the beef tenderloin generously with salt and pepper.
3. Rub the minced garlic and olive oil evenly over the surface of the tenderloin. Place the fresh thyme sprigs on top of the tenderloin.
4. Place the seasoned tenderloin in a sous vide bag, removing any air and sealing it tightly.
5. Once the water bath reaches the desired temperature, submerge the bag containing the tenderloin into the water.
6. Cook the tenderloin for 1 hour, ensuring it is fully submerged throughout the cooking process.
7. After cooking, remove the tenderloin from the sous vide bag and pat it dry with paper towels.
8. Optional step: Preheat a skillet over high heat and add butter. Sear the tenderloin for 1-2 minutes on each side until a golden crust forms.

Nutritional information: Approximately 400 calories, 50g protein, 0g carbohydrates, 20g fat, 0g fiber, 150mg cholesterol, 100mg sodium, 700mg potassium per serving.

Sous Vide Beef Stew

Yield: 4 servings | Prep Time: 20 minutes | Cook Time: 24 hours

Ingredients:

- 1.5 pounds of beef stew meat, cubed
- Salt and pepper, to taste
- 2 tablespoons all-purpose flour
- 2 tablespoons olive oil
- 2 cloves garlic, minced
- 1 onion, diced
- 2 carrots, diced
- 2 stalks celery, diced
- 2 cups beef broth

- 1 cup red wine (optional)
- 2 bay leaves
- 1 teaspoon dried thyme
- 1 teaspoon dried rosemary
- 1 cup frozen peas (optional)
- Chopped fresh parsley, for garnish (optional)

Directions:

1. Season the beef stew meat with salt and pepper, then coat it evenly with flour.
2. Heat the olive oil in a large skillet over medium-high heat. Brown the beef cubes on all sides, working in batches if necessary. Transfer the browned beef to a plate. In the same skillet, add the minced garlic, diced onion, carrots, and celery. Cook until softened, about 5 minutes.
3. Transfer the cooked vegetables to a sous vide bag. Add the browned beef cubes, beef broth, red wine (if using), bay leaves, dried thyme, and dried rosemary to the bag.
4. Remove any air from the bag and seal it tightly.
5. Preheat the sous vide water bath to 155°F (68°C) and cook the beef stew for 24 hours.
6. About 30 minutes before serving, heat a skillet over medium heat and sauté the frozen peas until heated through.
7. Remove the beef stew from the sous vide bath, open the bag, and transfer the contents to a serving dish. Discard the bay leaves.
8. Optional step: Garnish with sautéed peas and chopped fresh parsley before serving.

Nutritional information: Approximately 400 calories, 35g protein, 15g carbohydrates, 20g fat, 3g fiber, 90mg cholesterol, 800mg sodium, 700mg potassium per serving.

Sous Vide Beef Wellington

Yield: 4 servings | Prep Time: 30 minutes | Cook Time: 1 hour

Ingredients:

- 4 beef tenderloin fillets, about 6 ounces each
- Salt and pepper, to taste
- 2 tablespoons olive oil
- 1 tablespoon Dijon mustard
- 8 slices prosciutto
- 1 sheet puff pastry, thawed
- 1 egg, beaten (for egg wash)
- 2 tablespoons butter
- 8 ounces mushrooms, finely chopped
- 2 cloves garlic, minced
- 1/4 cup chopped fresh parsley
- Salt and pepper, to taste
- 1/4 cup dry white wine
- 1/4 cup beef broth

Directions:

1. Preheat the sous vide water bath to 130°F (54°C) for medium-rare beef tenderloin.
2. Season the beef tenderloin fillets with salt and pepper. Brush each fillet with Dijon mustard.
3. Wrap each fillet with 2 slices of prosciutto, ensuring they are fully covered. Place the wrapped fillets in sous vide bags, drizzle with olive oil, and seal the bags tightly.
4. Once the water bath reaches the desired temperature, immerse the bags containing the fillets into the water. Cook for 1 hour.
5. While the beef is cooking, prepare the mushroom duxelles. In a skillet, melt butter over medium heat. Add minced garlic and chopped mushrooms. Cook until the mushrooms release their moisture and become golden brown, about 8-10 minutes. Stir in chopped parsley and season with salt and pepper. Deglaze the skillet with white wine and beef broth, simmering until the liquid has evaporated. Set aside to cool.
6. Preheat the oven to 400°F (200°C).
7. Roll out the puff pastry sheet on a floured surface. Cut it into four equal squares.
8. Place a spoonful of mushroom duxelles in the center of each puff pastry square.
9. Once the beef fillets are done cooking, remove them from the sous vide bags and pat them dry with paper towels.
10. Place a beef fillet on top of the mushroom duxelles on each puff pastry square.
11. Fold the puff pastry over the beef, sealing the edges. Trim any excess pastry if necessary.
12. Brush the tops of the puff pastry with beaten egg for an egg wash.
13. Place the beef Wellingtons on a baking sheet lined with parchment paper and bake for 20-25 minutes, or until the pastry is golden brown and crispy.
14. Serve hot, garnished with additional parsley if desired.

Nutritional information: Approximately 700 calories, 40g protein, 30g carbohydrates, 45g fat, 2g fiber, 160mg cholesterol, 900mg sodium, 600mg potassium per serving.

Sous Vide Beef Tacos

Yield: 4 servings | Prep Time: 15 minutes | Cook Time: 2 hours

Ingredients:

- 1.5 pounds beef chuck roast, cut into chunks
- Salt and pepper, to taste
- 2 tablespoons olive oil
- 2 cloves garlic, minced
- 1 onion, diced
- 1 tablespoon chili powder
- 1 teaspoon ground cumin
- 1 teaspoon paprika
- 1/2 teaspoon dried oregano
- 1 cup beef broth
- 8 small flour or corn tortillas
- Toppings: shredded lettuce, diced tomatoes, diced onions, shredded cheese, salsa, sour cream, cilantro, lime wedges, etc.

Directions:

1. Preheat the sous vide water bath to 165°F (74°C).
2. Season the beef chuck roast chunks with salt and pepper.
3. In a large skillet, heat the olive oil over medium-high heat. Brown the beef chunks on all sides, working in batches if necessary. Transfer the browned beef to a plate. In the same skillet, add minced garlic and diced onion. Cook until softened, about 5 minutes.
4. Add chili powder, ground cumin, paprika, and dried oregano to the skillet. Cook for another minute until fragrant.
5. Deglaze the skillet with beef broth, scraping up any browned bits from the bottom of the pan. Bring to a simmer.
6. Transfer the beef, onions, and spices to a sous vide bag. Remove any air from the bag and seal it tightly. Once the water bath reaches the desired temperature, submerge the bag containing the beef into the water.
7. Cook the beef sous vide for 2 hours.
8. After cooking, remove the beef from the sous vide bag and shred it using forks.
9. Warm the tortillas in a dry skillet or microwave.
10. Assemble the tacos by placing a spoonful of shredded beef onto each tortilla. Top with desired toppings.
11. Serve hot with lime wedges on the side.

Nutritional information: Approximately 350 calories, 25g protein, 20g carbohydrates, 18g fat, 2g fiber, 70mg cholesterol, 800mg sodium, 500mg potassium per serving.

Sous Vide Beef Bulgogi

Yield: 4 servings | Prep Time: 15 minutes | Cook Time: 2 hours

Ingredients:

- 1.5 pounds beef sirloin, thinly sliced
- 1/2 cup soy sauce
- 1/4 cup brown sugar
- 2 tablespoons sesame oil
- 2 tablespoons rice vinegar
- 4 cloves garlic, minced
- 1 tablespoon grated fresh ginger
- 2 green onions, thinly sliced
- 1 tablespoon toasted sesame seeds
- Optional: sliced mushrooms, bell peppers, or onions for serving

Directions:

1. In a bowl, combine soy sauce, brown sugar, sesame oil, rice vinegar, minced garlic, grated ginger, sliced green onions, and toasted sesame seeds to make the marinade.
2. Place the thinly sliced beef sirloin in a resealable plastic bag or vacuum-sealed bag.
3. Pour the marinade over the beef, ensuring it is evenly coated. Seal the bag tightly and massage the marinade into the beef. Refrigerate the marinated beef for at least 1 hour, or overnight for the best flavor.
4. Preheat the sous vide water bath to 140°F (60°C).

5. Once the beef has marinated, remove it from the refrigerator and transfer it to a sous vide bag, removing any excess marinade.
6. Seal the bag tightly and place it in the preheated water bath. Cook the beef for 2 hours.
7. After cooking, remove the bag from the water bath and carefully open it.
8. Optionally, sear the beef slices in a hot skillet or grill for a few seconds on each side to caramelize.
9. Serve the sous vide beef bulgogi hot with rice and your choice of sliced mushrooms, bell peppers, or onions.

Nutritional information: Approximately 300 calories, 30g protein, 15g carbohydrates, 12g fat, 1g fiber, 70mg cholesterol, 1200mg sodium, 400mg potassium per serving.

Sous Vide Beef Stir-Fry

Yield: 4 servings | Prep Time: 15 minutes | Cook Time: 1 hour

Ingredients:

- 1.5 pounds beef sirloin, thinly sliced
- Salt and pepper, to taste
- 3 tablespoons soy sauce
- 2 tablespoons oyster sauce
- 2 tablespoons rice vinegar
- 2 tablespoons brown sugar
- 1 tablespoon sesame oil
- 2 cloves garlic, minced
- 1 tablespoon grated fresh ginger
- 1 tablespoon cornstarch
- 2 tablespoons vegetable oil
- 1 onion, thinly sliced
- 2 bell peppers, thinly sliced
- 1 cup broccoli florets
- Optional: sliced mushrooms, snap peas, or carrots
- Cooked rice, for serving
- Sesame seeds and sliced green onions, for garnish

Directions:

1. Season the thinly sliced beef sirloin with salt and pepper.
2. In a bowl, whisk together soy sauce, oyster sauce, rice vinegar, brown sugar, sesame oil, minced garlic, grated ginger, and cornstarch to make the marinade.
3. Place the beef slices in a resealable plastic bag or vacuum-sealed bag.
4. Pour the marinade over the beef, ensuring it is evenly coated. Seal the bag tightly and massage the marinade into the beef.
5. Refrigerate the marinated beef for at least 30 minutes.
6. Preheat the sous vide water bath to 130°F (54°C).
7. Once the beef has marinated, remove it from the refrigerator and transfer it to a sous vide bag, removing any excess marinade.

8. Seal the bag tightly and place it in the preheated water bath. Cook the beef for 1 hour.
9. After cooking, remove the bag from the water bath and carefully open it. Remove the beef from the bag and pat it dry with paper towels.
10. Heat vegetable oil in a large skillet or wok over high heat. Add the thinly sliced onion, bell peppers, broccoli florets, and any optional vegetables. Stir-fry for 3-4 minutes until vegetables are crisp-tender.
11. Add the sous vide beef slices to the skillet and stir-fry for an additional 2-3 minutes until heated through.
12. Serve the beef stir-fry hot overcooked rice, garnished with sesame seeds and sliced green onions.

Nutritional information: Approximately 400 calories, 35g protein, 20g carbohydrates, 18g fat, 3g fiber, 70mg cholesterol, 1000mg sodium, 600mg potassium per serving.

Sous Vide Beef Sausages

Yield: 4 servings | Prep Time: 10 minutes | Cook Time: 2 hours
Ingredients:

- 4 beef sausages
- Salt and pepper, to taste
- Optional: herbs and spices of your choice

Directions:

1. Preheat the sous vide water bath to 140°F (60°C).
2. Season the beef sausages with salt, pepper, and any desired herbs or spices.
3. Place the seasoned sausages in a large resealable plastic bag or vacuum-sealed bag.
4. Once the water bath reaches the desired temperature, submerge the bag containing the sausages into the water.
5. Cook the beef sausages sous vide for 2 hours.
6. After cooking, remove the bag from the water bath and carefully open it.
7. Remove the sausages from the bag and pat them dry with paper towels.
8. Optionally, sear the sausages on a preheated grill or skillet for 1-2 minutes on each side to achieve a golden brown color and crisp exterior.
9. Serve the sous vide beef sausages hot with your favorite sides and condiments.

Nutritional information: Approximately 300 calories, 15g protein, 2g carbohydrates, 25g fat, 0g fiber, 70mg cholesterol, 600mg sodium, 200mg potassium per serving.

Pork Recipes

Sous Vide Pork Tenderloin

Yield: 4 servings | Prep Time: 10 minutes | Cook Time: 1 hour

Ingredients:

- 2 pork tenderloins, about 1 pound each
- Salt and pepper, to taste
- 2 tablespoons olive oil
- 4 cloves garlic, minced
- 2 tablespoons fresh rosemary, chopped

- 2 tablespoons fresh thyme, chopped
- 2 tablespoons Dijon mustard
- 2 tablespoons honey
- 2 tablespoons balsamic vinegar
- Optional: additional herbs for garnish

Directions:

1. Preheat the sous vide water bath to 140°F (60°C).
2. Season the pork tenderloins generously with salt and pepper.
3. In a small bowl, mix olive oil, minced garlic, chopped rosemary, chopped thyme, Dijon mustard, honey, and balsamic vinegar to create the marinade.
4. Rub the marinade evenly over the pork tenderloins, ensuring they are well coated.
5. Place each pork tenderloin in a separate sous vide bag, removing any air and sealing them tightly.
6. Once the water bath reaches the desired temperature, submerge the bags containing the pork tenderloins into the water.
7. Cook the pork tenderloins for 1 hour.
8. After cooking, remove the bags from the water bath and carefully open them.
9. Remove the pork tenderloins from the bags and pat them dry with paper towels.
10. Optional step: Preheat a skillet over high heat and sear the pork tenderloins for 1-2 minutes on each side for a golden crust.
11. Let the pork tenderloins rest for a few minutes before slicing.
12. Garnish with additional herbs if desired and serve hot.

Nutritional information: Approximately 250 calories, 30g protein, 5g carbohydrates, 12g fat, 0g fiber, 80mg cholesterol, 300mg sodium, 400mg potassium per serving.

Sous Vide Pork Chops

Yield: 4 servings | Prep Time: 10 minutes | Cook Time: 2 hours

Ingredients:

- 4 bone-in pork chops, about 1 inch thick
- Salt and pepper, to taste
- 2 tablespoons olive oil
- 4 cloves garlic, minced
- 2 tablespoons fresh thyme, chopped
- 2 tablespoons fresh rosemary, chopped
- 2 tablespoons balsamic vinegar
- 2 tablespoons honey
- Optional: additional herbs for garnish

Directions:

1. Preheat the sous vide water bath to 140°F (60°C).
2. Season the pork chops generously with salt and pepper.

3. In a small bowl, mix olive oil, minced garlic, chopped thyme, chopped rosemary, balsamic vinegar, and honey to create the marinade.
4. Rub the marinade evenly over the pork chops, ensuring they are well coated.
5. Place each pork chop in a separate sous vide bag, removing any air and sealing them tightly.
6. Once the water bath reaches the desired temperature, submerge the bags containing the pork chops into the water.
7. Cook the pork chops for 2 hours.
8. After cooking, remove the bags from the water bath and carefully open them.
9. Remove the pork chops from the bags and pat them dry with paper towels.
10. Optional step: Preheat a skillet over high heat and sear the pork chops for 1-2 minutes on each side for a golden crust.
11. Let the pork chops rest for a few minutes before serving.
12. Garnish with additional herbs if desired and serve hot.

Nutritional information: Approximately 300 calories, 25g protein, 10g carbohydrates, 15g fat, 0g fiber, 80mg cholesterol, 300mg sodium, 400mg potassium per serving.

Sous Vide Pork Belly

Yield: 4 servings | Prep Time: 15 minutes | Cook Time: 12 hours

Ingredients:

- 2 pounds pork belly, skin removed and cut into 2-inch cubes
- Salt and pepper, to taste
- 2 tablespoons soy sauce
- 2 tablespoons hoisin sauce
- 2 tablespoons honey
- 2 tablespoons rice vinegar
- 4 cloves garlic, minced
- 1 tablespoon grated fresh ginger
- 1 tablespoon sesame oil

Directions:

1. Preheat the sous vide water bath to 165°F (74°C).
2. Season the pork belly cubes with salt and pepper.
3. In a bowl, mix soy sauce, hoisin sauce, honey, rice vinegar, minced garlic, grated ginger, and sesame oil to make the marinade.
4. Place the pork belly cubes in a resealable plastic bag or vacuum-sealed bag.
5. Pour the marinade over the pork belly cubes, ensuring they are evenly coated. Seal the bag tightly.
6. Once the water bath reaches the desired temperature, submerge the bag containing the pork belly into the water.
7. Cook the pork belly sous vide for 12 hours.
8. After cooking, remove the bag from the water bath and carefully open it.
9. Remove the pork belly cubes from the bag and pat them dry with paper towels.
10. Preheat a skillet over medium-high heat. Sear the pork belly cubes for 1-2 minutes on each side until golden brown and crispy.

11. Serve the sous vide pork belly hot, garnished with sesame seeds and sliced green onions if desired.

Nutritional information: Approximately 400 calories, 20g protein, 5g carbohydrates, 35g fat, 0g fiber, 90mg cholesterol, 800mg sodium, 300mg potassium per serving.

Sous Vide Pulled Pork

Yield: 6 servings | Prep Time: 10 minutes | Cook Time: 12 hours

Ingredients:

- 3 pounds pork shoulder or pork butt, boneless
- Salt and pepper, to taste
- 2 tablespoons brown sugar
- 2 tablespoons paprika
- 1 tablespoon garlic powder
- 1 tablespoon onion powder
- 1 teaspoon cayenne pepper (adjust to taste)
- 1 cup barbecue sauce
- Optional: buns, coleslaw, pickles, for serving

Directions:

1. Preheat the sous vide water bath to 165°F (74°C).
2. Season the pork shoulder or pork butt with salt and pepper.
3. In a small bowl, mix brown sugar, paprika, garlic powder, onion powder, and cayenne pepper to create a dry rub.
4. Rub the dry rub mixture evenly over the pork shoulder or pork butt.
5. Place the seasoned pork in a large resealable plastic bag or vacuum-sealed bag.
6. Pour barbecue sauce over the pork, ensuring it is evenly coated. Seal the bag tightly.
7. Once the water bath reaches the desired temperature, submerge the bag containing the pork into the water.
8. Cook the pork sous vide for 12 hours.
9. After cooking, remove the bag from the water bath and carefully open it.
10. Remove the pork from the bag and transfer it to a large bowl. Use two forks to shred the pork.
11. Serve the sous vide pulled pork hot on buns with coleslaw and pickles, if desired.

Nutritional information: Approximately 400 calories, 30g protein, 15g carbohydrates, 25g fat, 1g fiber, 90mg cholesterol, 800mg sodium, 500mg potassium per serving.

Sous Vide Pork Ribs

Yield: 4 servings | Prep Time: 10 minutes | Cook Time: 18 hours

Ingredients:

- 2 racks of pork ribs

- Salt and pepper, to taste
- 1 cup barbecue sauce
- Optional: additional dry rub seasoning

Directions:

1. Preheat the sous vide water bath to 165°F (74°C).
2. Season the racks of pork ribs generously with salt and pepper. Optionally, rub them with your favorite dry rub seasoning.
3. Place each rack of ribs in a separate large resealable plastic bag or vacuum-sealed bag.
4. Pour barbecue sauce evenly over each rack of ribs, ensuring they are well coated. Seal the bags tightly.
5. Once the water bath reaches the desired temperature, submerge the bags containing the ribs into the water.
6. Cook the pork ribs sous vide for 18 hours.
7. After cooking, remove the bags from the water bath and carefully open them.
8. Remove the ribs from the bags and transfer them to a preheated grill or oven.
9. Grill or broil the ribs for 5-10 minutes on each side until they are nicely browned and caramelized.
10. Slice the ribs between the bones and serve hot with additional barbecue sauce on the side, if desired.

Nutritional information: Approximately 400 calories, 25g protein, 15g carbohydrates, 30g fat, 0g fiber, 90mg cholesterol, 800mg sodium, 300mg potassium per serving.

Sous Vide Pork Loin

Yield: 4 servings | Prep Time: 10 minutes | Cook Time: 2 hours

Ingredients:

- 2 pounds pork loin
- Salt and pepper, to taste
- 2 tablespoons olive oil
- 4 cloves garlic, minced
- 2 tablespoons fresh rosemary, chopped
- 2 tablespoons fresh thyme, chopped
- 2 tablespoons balsamic vinegar
- 2 tablespoons honey

Directions:

1. Preheat the sous vide water bath to 140°F (60°C).
2. Season the pork loin with salt and pepper.
3. In a small bowl, mix olive oil, minced garlic, chopped rosemary, chopped thyme, balsamic vinegar, and honey.
4. Rub the mixture evenly over the pork loin, ensuring it is well coated.
5. Place the pork loin in a large resealable plastic bag or vacuum-sealed bag.
6. Once the water bath reaches the desired temperature, submerge the bag containing the pork loin into the water.
7. Cook the pork loin sous vide for 2 hours.
8. After cooking, remove the bag from the water bath and carefully open it.
9. Remove the pork loin from the bag and pat it dry with paper towels.

10. Preheat a skillet over medium-high heat. Sear the pork loin for 1-2 minutes on each side until golden brown.
11. Let the pork loin rest for a few minutes before slicing.
12. Serve the sous vide pork loin hot, garnished with additional herbs if desired.

Nutritional information: Approximately 250 calories, 30g protein, 5g carbohydrates, 12g fat, 0g fiber, 80mg cholesterol, 300mg sodium, 400mg potassium per serving.

Sous Vide Pork Carnitas

Yield: 4 servings | Prep Time: 10 minutes | Cook Time: 12 hours

Ingredients:

- 2 pounds pork shoulder or pork butt, cut into large chunks
- Salt and pepper, to taste
- 2 tablespoons olive oil
- 1 onion, finely chopped
- 4 cloves garlic, minced
- 2 teaspoons ground cumin
- 2 teaspoons chili powder
- 1 teaspoon dried oregano
- 1 teaspoon smoked paprika
- 1 cup orange juice
- 1/2 cup lime juice
- 1/4 cup chopped fresh cilantro
- Optional: tortillas, diced onions, chopped cilantro, lime wedges for serving

Directions:

1. Preheat the sous vide water bath to 165°F (74°C).
2. Season the pork chunks with salt and pepper.
3. In a large skillet, heat olive oil over medium heat. Add the chopped onion and cook until softened about 5 minutes.
4. Add minced garlic, ground cumin, chili powder, dried oregano, and smoked paprika to the skillet. Cook for another minute until fragrant.
5. Transfer the onion and spice mixture to a large resealable plastic bag or vacuum-sealed bag.
6. Add the seasoned pork chunks to the bag with the onion and spice mixture.
7. Pour orange juice and lime juice over the pork chunks. Add chopped cilantro to the bag. Seal the bag tightly.
8. Once the water bath reaches the desired temperature, submerge the bag containing the pork into the water.
9. Cook the pork sous vide for 12 hours.
10. After cooking, remove the bag from the water bath and carefully open it.
11. Remove the pork chunks from the bag and transfer them to a baking sheet lined with aluminum foil. Use forks to shred the pork into smaller pieces.
12. Preheat the broiler. Place the baking sheet with the shredded pork under the broiler for 5-7 minutes, or until the edges are crispy.
13. Serve the sous vide pork carnitas hot, with tortillas and your choice of toppings.

Nutritional information: Approximately 350 calories, 25g protein, 10g carbohydrates, 20g fat, 2g fiber, 80mg cholesterol, 500mg sodium, 400mg potassium per serving.

Sous Vide Pork Ramen

Yield: 4 servings | Prep Time: 20 minutes | Cook Time: 12 hours

Ingredients:

- 1 pound pork belly, sliced
- Salt and pepper, to taste
- 2 tablespoons soy sauce
- 2 tablespoons mirin
- 2 tablespoons sake (optional)
- 2 tablespoons brown sugar
- 4 cloves garlic, minced
- 1 tablespoon grated fresh ginger
- 6 cups chicken or pork broth
- 4 portions of ramen noodles
- 4 soft-boiled eggs
- 2 cups sliced mushrooms (shiitake, button, or oyster)
- 2 cups baby spinach
- 4 green onions, sliced
- Optional toppings: nori sheets, bamboo shoots, corn kernels, sesame seeds

Directions:

1. Preheat the sous vide water bath to 165°F (74°C).
2. Season the pork belly slices with salt and pepper.
3. In a bowl, mix soy sauce, mirin, sake (if using), brown sugar, minced garlic, and grated ginger to create the marinade.
4. Place the pork belly slices in a large resealable plastic bag or vacuum-sealed bag.
5. Pour the marinade over the pork belly slices, ensuring they are well coated. Seal the bag tightly.
6. Once the water bath reaches the desired temperature, submerge the bag containing the pork into the water.
7. Cook the pork sous vide for 12 hours.
8. After cooking, remove the bag from the water bath and carefully open it.
9. Remove the pork belly slices from the bag and pat them dry with paper towels. Slice them thinly.
10. In a large pot, bring the chicken or pork broth to a simmer. Add sliced mushrooms and baby spinach. Cook for 5 minutes.
11. Cook the ramen noodles according to the package instructions. Divide the cooked ramen noodles among serving bowls. Ladle the hot broth with mushrooms and spinach over the noodles.
12. Arrange the sliced sous vide pork belly, soft-boiled eggs, and sliced green onions on top of the ramen.
13. Garnish with optional toppings like nori sheets, bamboo shoots, corn kernels, and sesame seeds.
14. Serve the sous vide pork ramen hot and enjoy!

Nutritional information: Approximately 600 calories, 30g protein, 40g carbohydrates, 35g fat, 5g fiber, 150mg cholesterol, 1500mg sodium, 600mg potassium per serving.

Sous Vide Pork Stir-Fry

Yield: 4 servings | Prep Time: 15 minutes | Cook Time: 1 hour

Ingredients:

- 1 pound pork loin, thinly sliced
- Salt and pepper, to taste
- 2 tablespoons soy sauce
- 1 tablespoon rice vinegar
- 1 tablespoon honey
- 1 teaspoon sesame oil
- 2 cloves garlic, minced
- 1 tablespoon grated fresh ginger
- 2 tablespoons vegetable oil
- 1 onion, sliced
- 2 bell peppers, sliced
- 1 cup broccoli florets
- 1 cup snap peas
- Cooked rice or noodles, for serving

Directions:

1. Preheat the sous vide water bath to 140°F (60°C).
2. Season the thinly sliced pork loin with salt and pepper.
3. In a bowl, mix soy sauce, rice vinegar, honey, sesame oil, minced garlic, and grated ginger to create the marinade.
4. Place the pork slices in a large resealable plastic bag or vacuum-sealed bag.
5. Pour the marinade over the pork slices, ensuring they are well coated. Seal the bag tightly.
6. Once the water bath reaches the desired temperature, submerge the bag containing the pork into the water.
7. Cook the pork sous vide for 1 hour.
8. After cooking, remove the bag from the water bath and carefully open it.
9. Heat vegetable oil in a large skillet or wok over high heat.
10. Add sliced onion, bell peppers, broccoli florets, and snap peas to the skillet. Stir-fry for 5-7 minutes until the vegetables are tender-crisp.
11. Remove the vegetables from the skillet and set aside. Add the sous vide pork slices to the skillet and stir-fry for 2-3 minutes until browned and heated through.
12. Return the cooked vegetables to the skillet and toss with the pork slices.
13. Serve the sous vide pork stir-fry hot cooked rice or noodles.

Nutritional information: Approximately 350 calories, 25g protein, 20g carbohydrates, 18g fat, 3g fiber, 70mg cholesterol, 800mg sodium, 500mg potassium per serving.

Sous Vide Pork Sausages

Yield: 4 servings | Prep Time: 5 minutes | Cook Time: 2 hours

Ingredients:

- 4 pork sausages
- Salt and pepper, to taste
- Optional: herbs and spices of your choice

Directions:

1. Preheat the sous vide water bath to 140°F (60°C).
2. Season the pork sausages with salt, pepper, and any herbs or spices of your choice.
3. Place the seasoned sausages in a large resealable plastic bag or vacuum-sealed bag.
4. Once the water bath reaches the desired temperature, submerge the bag containing the sausages into the water.
5. Cook the pork sausages sous vide for 2 hours.
6. After cooking, remove the bag from the water bath and carefully open it.
7. Remove the sausages from the bag and pat them dry with paper towels.
8. Optionally, sear the sausages on a preheated grill or skillet for 1-2 minutes on each side to achieve a golden brown color and crisp exterior.
9. Serve the sous vide pork sausages hot with your favorite sides and condiments.

Nutritional information: Approximately 250 calories, 15g protein, 2g carbohydrates, 20g fat, 0g fiber, 60mg cholesterol, 600mg sodium, 200mg potassium per serving.

Lamb and Game Meats

Sous Vide Lamb Chops

Yield: 4 servings | Prep Time: 10 minutes | Cook Time: 1 hour

Ingredients:

- 8 lamb chops, about 1 inch thick
- Salt and pepper, to taste
- 2 cloves garlic, minced
- 2 sprigs of fresh rosemary
- 2 sprigs of fresh thyme
- 2 tablespoons olive oil

Directions:

1. Preheat the sous vide water bath to 135°F (57°C) for medium-rare or 145°F (63°C) for medium doneness.
2. Season the lamb chops generously with salt and pepper on both sides.
3. Divide the minced garlic, rosemary, and thyme evenly among the lamb chops, pressing them onto the surface of each chop.
4. Place the seasoned lamb chops in a single layer in a large resealable plastic bag or vacuum-sealed bag.

5. Drizzle the olive oil over the lamb chops, ensuring they are well coated.
6. Seal the bag tightly, removing as much air as possible.
7. Once the water bath reaches the desired temperature, submerge the bag containing the lamb chops into the water.
8. Cook the lamb chops sous vide for 1 hour.
9. After cooking, remove the bag from the water bath and carefully open it.
10. Remove the lamb chops from the bag and pat them dry with paper towels.
11. Heat a skillet over high heat. Sear the lamb chops for 1-2 minutes on each side until browned and caramelized.
12. Serve the sous vide lamb chops hot, garnished with additional fresh herbs if desired.

Nutritional information: Approximately 300 calories, 30g protein, 0g carbohydrates, 20g fat, 0g fiber, 90mg cholesterol, 100mg sodium, 250mg potassium per serving.

Sous Vide Lamb Shoulder

Yield: 4 servings | Prep Time: 15 minutes | Cook Time: 18 hours

Ingredients:

- 2-3 pounds lamb shoulder, bone-in
- Salt and pepper, to taste
- 4 cloves garlic, minced
- 2 tablespoons fresh rosemary, chopped
- 2 tablespoons fresh thyme leaves
- 2 tablespoons olive oil

Directions:

1. Preheat the sous vide water bath to 155°F (68°C).
2. Season the lamb shoulder generously with salt and pepper on all sides.
3. Rub minced garlic, chopped rosemary, and thyme leaves over the lamb shoulder, ensuring it is evenly coated.
4. Place the seasoned lamb shoulder in a large resealable plastic bag or vacuum-sealed bag.
5. Drizzle olive oil over the lamb shoulder and seal the bag tightly, removing as much air as possible.
6. Once the water bath reaches the desired temperature, submerge the bag containing the lamb shoulder into the water.
7. Cook the lamb shoulder sous vide for 18 hours.
8. After cooking, remove the bag from the water bath and carefully open it.
9. Remove the lamb shoulder from the bag and pat it dry with paper towels.
10. Preheat a grill or skillet over high heat.
11. Sear the lamb shoulder for 2-3 minutes on each side until nicely browned and caramelized.
12. Let the lamb shoulder rest for a few minutes before slicing.
13. Serve the sous vide lamb shoulder hot, garnished with additional fresh herbs if desired.

Nutritional information: Approximately 400 calories, 40g protein, 0g carbohydrates, 25g fat, 0g fiber, 120mg cholesterol, 100mg sodium, 450mg potassium per serving.

Sous Vide Lamb Shank

Yield: 4 servings | Prep Time: 15 minutes | Cook Time: 24 hours

Ingredients:

- 4 lamb shanks
- Salt and pepper, to taste

- 4 cloves garlic, minced
- 2 tablespoons fresh rosemary, chopped
- 2 tablespoons fresh thyme leaves
- 2 tablespoons olive oil

Directions:

1. Preheat the sous vide water bath to 160°F (71°C).
2. Season the lamb shanks generously with salt and pepper on all sides.
3. Rub minced garlic, chopped rosemary, and thyme leaves over each lamb shank, ensuring they are evenly coated.
4. Place each seasoned lamb shank in individual large resealable plastic bags or vacuum-sealed bags.
5. Drizzle olive oil over each lamb shank and seal the bags tightly, removing as much air as possible.
6. Once the water bath reaches the desired temperature, submerge the bags containing the lamb shanks into the water.
7. Cook the lamb shanks sous vide for 24 hours.
8. After cooking, remove the bags from the water bath and carefully open them. Remove the lamb shanks from the bags and pat them dry with paper towels.
9. Preheat a grill or skillet over high heat. Sear the lamb shanks for 2-3 minutes on each side until nicely browned and caramelized.
10. Let the lamb shanks rest for a few minutes before serving.
11. Serve the sous vide lamb shanks hot, garnished with additional fresh herbs if desired.

Nutritional information: Approximately 500 calories, 50g protein, 0g carbohydrates, 30g fat, 0g fiber, 150mg cholesterol, 120mg sodium, 550mg potassium per serving

Sous Vide Rack of Lamb

Yield: 2 servings | Prep Time: 15 minutes | Cook Time: 1 hour

Ingredients:

- 1 rack of lamb, frenched (about 1.5 pounds)
- Salt and pepper, to taste
- 2 cloves garlic, minced
- 2 tablespoons fresh rosemary, chopped
- 2 tablespoons olive oil

Directions:

1. Preheat the sous vide water bath to 130°F (54°C) for medium-rare or 140°F (60°C) for medium doneness.
2. Season the rack of lamb generously with salt and pepper on all sides.
3. Rub minced garlic and chopped rosemary over the rack of lamb, ensuring it is evenly coated.
4. Place the seasoned rack of lamb in a large resealable plastic bag or vacuum-sealed bag.
5. Drizzle olive oil over the rack of lamb and seal the bag tightly, removing as much air as possible.
6. Once the water bath reaches the desired temperature, submerge the bag containing the rack of lamb into the water.
7. Cook the rack of lamb sous vide for 1 hour.
8. After cooking, remove the bag from the water bath and carefully open it. Remove the rack of lamb from the bag and pat it dry with paper towels.
9. Preheat a grill or skillet over high heat.
10. Sear the rack of lamb for 1-2 minutes on each side until nicely browned and caramelized.
11. Let the rack of lamb rest for a few minutes before slicing into individual chops.
12. Serve the sous vide rack of lamb hot, garnished with additional fresh rosemary if desired.

Nutritional information: Approximately 400 calories, 40g protein, 0g carbohydrates, 25g fat, 0g fiber, 100mg cholesterol, 100mg sodium, 300mg potassium per serving.

Sous Vide Lamb Leg

Yield: 4 servings | Prep Time: 15 minutes | Cook Time: 6 hours

Ingredients:

- 1 bone-in leg of lamb, about 4-5 pounds
- Salt and pepper, to taste
- 4 cloves garlic, minced
- 2 tablespoons fresh rosemary, chopped
- 2 tablespoons fresh thyme leaves
- 2 tablespoons olive oil

Directions:

1. Preheat the sous vide water bath to 135°F (57°C) for medium-rare or 145°F (63°C) for medium doneness.
2. Season the lamb leg generously with salt and pepper on all sides.
3. Rub minced garlic, chopped rosemary, and thyme leaves over the lamb leg, ensuring it is evenly coated.
4. Place the seasoned lamb leg in a large resealable plastic bag or vacuum-sealed bag.
5. Drizzle olive oil over the lamb leg and seal the bag tightly, removing as much air as possible.
6. Once the water bath reaches the desired temperature, submerge the bag containing the lamb leg into the water.
7. Cook the lamb leg sous vide for 6 hours.
8. After cooking, remove the bag from the water bath and carefully open it. Remove the lamb leg from the bag and pat it dry with paper towels.
9. Preheat a grill or skillet over high heat.
10. Sear the lamb leg for 2-3 minutes on each side until nicely browned and caramelized.
11. Let the lamb leg rest for a few minutes before slicing.
12. Serve the sous vide lamb leg hot, garnished with additional fresh herbs if desired.

Nutritional information: Approximately 350 calories, 50g protein, 0g carbohydrates, 15g fat, 0g fiber, 160mg cholesterol, 100mg sodium, 500mg potassium per serving.

Sous Vide Lamb Sausages

Yield: 4 servings | Prep Time: 15 minutes | Cook Time: 2 hours

Ingredients:

- 1 pound ground lamb
- 1 teaspoon salt
- 1 teaspoon black pepper
- 1 teaspoon ground cumin
- 1 teaspoon paprika
- 1 teaspoon garlic powder
- 1 teaspoon onion powder
- 1 teaspoon dried oregano
- 1 teaspoon dried thyme
- 1/4 teaspoon cayenne pepper (optional)
- Natural lamb casings (optional)

Directions:

1. In a mixing bowl, combine ground lamb with salt, black pepper, ground cumin, paprika, garlic powder, onion powder, dried oregano, dried thyme, and cayenne pepper if using. Mix well until all the spices are evenly distributed throughout the meat. If using natural lamb casings, rinse them thoroughly under cold water and soak them in warm water for about 30 minutes to soften.
2. Stuff the seasoned lamb mixture into the casings using a sausage stuffer or a piping bag fitted with a large tip. Twist the casings at regular intervals to form individual sausages. If not using casings, shape the seasoned lamb mixture into sausage shapes by hand. Vacuum seal the sausages in individual bags or place them in a single layer in a large resealable bag, removing as much air as possible.
3. Preheat the sous vide water bath to 145°F (63°C).
4. Once the water bath reaches the desired temperature, submerge the sealed bags of sausages into the water.
5. Cook the lamb sausages sous vide for 2 hours.
6. After cooking, remove the sausages from the water bath and let them cool slightly. If using casings, carefully remove them from the sausages.
7. Preheat a grill or skillet over medium-high heat.
8. Sear the sausages for 1-2 minutes on each side until browned and crispy.
9. Serve the sous vide lamb sausages hot with your favorite sides or use them in recipes.

Nutritional information: Approximately 300 calories, 20g protein, 2g carbohydrates, 24g fat, 0g fiber, 80mg cholesterol, 500mg sodium, 200mg potassium per serving.

Sous Vide Venison Tenderloin

Yield: 4 servings | Prep time: 10 minutes | Cook time: 2 hours

Ingredients:

- 2 venison tenderloins (about 1 pound each)
- Salt and pepper to taste
- 2 cloves garlic, minced
- 2 sprigs of fresh rosemary
- 2 tablespoons olive oil

Directions:

1. Preheat the sous vide water bath to 135°F (57°C).
2. Season venison tenderloins generously with salt, pepper, and minced garlic.
3. Place each tenderloin in a separate vacuum-sealed bag, along with a sprig of rosemary and a drizzle of olive oil.
4. Seal the bags using a vacuum sealer or the water displacement method.
5. Submerge the sealed bags in the preheated water bath and cook for 2 hours.
6. After 2 hours, remove the bags from the water bath and carefully open them.
7. Heat a skillet over high heat and sear the tenderloins for 1-2 minutes on each side until nicely browned.

Nutritional information: 320 calories, 48g protein, 0g carbohydrates, 14g fat, 0g fiber, 140mg cholesterol, 250mg sodium, 590mg potassium

Sous Vide Venison Backstrap

Yield: 4 servings | Prep time: 15 minutes | Cook time: 2 hours

Ingredients:

- 2 venison backstraps (about 1 pound each)
- Salt and pepper to taste
- 3 cloves garlic, minced
- 2 tablespoons balsamic vinegar
- 2 tablespoons olive oil
- 2 sprigs of fresh thyme

Directions:

1. Preheat the sous vide water bath to 135°F (57°C).
2. Season venison backstraps generously with salt, pepper, and minced garlic.
3. Place each backstrap in a separate vacuum-sealed bag, along with a sprig of thyme, balsamic vinegar, and olive oil.
4. Seal the bags using a vacuum sealer or the water displacement method.
5. Submerge the sealed bags in the preheated water bath and cook for 2 hours.
6. After 2 hours, remove the bags from the water bath and carefully open them.
7. Heat a skillet over high heat and sear the backstraps for 1-2 minutes on each side until nicely browned.

Nutritional information: 280 calories, 46g protein, 2g carbohydrates, 10g fat, 0g fiber, 140mg cholesterol, 180mg sodium, 510mg potassium

Sous Vide Wild Boar Shoulder

Yield: 4 servings | Prep time: 15 minutes | Cook time: 24 hours

Ingredients:

- 2 pounds wild boar shoulder, bone-in
- Salt and pepper to taste
- 4 cloves garlic, minced
- 2 sprigs of fresh thyme
- 2 tablespoons olive oil

Directions:

1. Preheat the sous vide water bath to 165°F (74°C).
2. Season the wild boar shoulder generously with salt, pepper, and minced garlic.
3. Place the shoulder in a large vacuum-sealed bag, along with fresh thyme and olive oil.
4. Seal the bag using a vacuum sealer or the water displacement method.
5. Submerge the sealed bag in the preheated water bath and cook for 24 hours.
6. After 24 hours, remove the bag from the water bath and carefully open it. Remove the wild boar shoulder from the bag and pat it dry with paper towels.
7. Heat a skillet over high heat and sear the shoulder for 2-3 minutes on each side until nicely browned.
8. Let the shoulder rest for a few minutes before slicing and serving.

Nutritional information: 320 calories, 48g protein, 0g carbohydrates, 14g fat, 0g fiber, 140mg cholesterol, 250mg sodium, 590mg potassium

Sous Vide Rabbit Confit

Yield: 4 servings | Prep time: 20 minutes | Cook time: 12 hours

Ingredients:

- 4 rabbit legs

- Salt and pepper to taste
- 4 cloves garlic, minced
- 4 sprigs of fresh thyme
- 1 cup duck fat (or substitute with olive oil)

Directions:

1. Preheat the sous vide water bath to 167°F (75°C).
2. Season rabbit legs generously with salt, pepper, and minced garlic.
3. Place each leg in a separate vacuum-sealed bag, along with a sprig of thyme and enough duck fat to cover.
4. Seal the bags using a vacuum sealer or the water displacement method.
5. Submerge the sealed bags in the preheated water bath and cook for 12 hours.
6. After 12 hours, remove the bags from the water bath and carefully open them. Remove the rabbit legs from the bags and pat them dry with paper towels.
7. Heat a skillet over medium-high heat and sear the legs for 2-3 minutes on each side until golden brown.
8. Serve the rabbit confit hot, garnished with fresh herbs if desired.

Nutritional information: 320 calories, 35g protein, 0g carbohydrates, 20g fat, 0g fiber, 160mg cholesterol, 400mg sodium, 300mg potassium

Sous Vide Moose Sirloin

Yield: 4 servings | Prep time: 10 minutes | Cook time: 2 hours

Ingredients:

- 2 pounds moose sirloin, trimmed
- 2 tablespoons olive oil
- 4 cloves garlic, minced
- 2 sprigs of fresh rosemary
- Salt and pepper to taste

Directions:

1. Preheat the sous vide water bath to 130°F (54°C).
2. Season the moose sirloin generously with salt and pepper.
3. Place the seasoned moose sirloin, minced garlic, and fresh rosemary in a vacuum-sealed bag. Drizzle with olive oil and seal the bag.
4. Once the water bath has reached the desired temperature, place the sealed bag in the water bath and cook for 2 hours.
5. After 2 hours, remove the bag from the water bath and take out the moose sirloin.
6. Preheat a skillet over high heat. Sear the moose sirloin on all sides until nicely browned, about 1 minute per side.
7. Let the moose sirloin rest for a few minutes before slicing. Serve hot and enjoy!

Nutritional information: (per serving) 320 calories, 50g protein, 2g carbohydrates, 12g fat, 0g fiber, 150mg cholesterol, 500mg sodium, 800mg potassium

Chapter 5 Poultry

Chicken

Sous Vide Chicken Breast

Yield: 4 servings | Prep time: 10 minutes | Cook time: 1 hour

Ingredients:

- 4 boneless, skinless chicken breasts
- 2 tablespoons olive oil
- 2 cloves garlic, minced
- 1 teaspoon dried thyme
- Salt and pepper to taste

Directions:

1. Preheat the sous vide water bath to 145°F (63°C).
2. Season the chicken breasts with salt, pepper, and dried thyme.
3. Place the seasoned chicken breasts, minced garlic, and olive oil in a vacuum-sealed bag. Remove as much air as possible and seal the bag.
4. Once the water bath has reached the desired temperature, place the sealed bag in the water bath and cook for 1 hour.
5. After 1 hour, remove the bag from the water bath and take out the chicken breasts.
6. Preheat a skillet over medium-high heat. Remove the chicken breasts from the bag and pat dry with paper towels. Sear the chicken breasts in the skillet for 1-2 minutes on each side until golden brown.
7. Serve the chicken breasts hot with your favorite side dishes and enjoy!

Nutritional information: (per serving) 250 calories, 50g protein, 0g carbohydrates, 7g fat, 0g fiber, 130mg cholesterol, 400mg sodium, 450mg potassium

Sous Vide Chicken Thighs

Yield: 4 servings | Prep time: 10 minutes | Cook time: 2 hours

Ingredients:

- 8 bone-in, skin-on chicken thighs
- 2 tablespoons olive oil
- 4 cloves garlic, minced
- 2 teaspoons dried rosemary
- Salt and pepper to taste

Directions:

1. Preheat the sous vide water bath to 165°F (74°C).
2. Season the chicken thighs with salt, pepper, and dried rosemary.
3. Place the seasoned chicken thighs, minced garlic, and olive oil in a vacuum-sealed bag. Remove as much air as possible and seal the bag.
4. Once the water bath has reached the desired temperature, place the sealed bag in the water bath and cook for 2 hours.
5. After 2 hours, remove the bag from the water bath and take out the chicken thighs.
6. Preheat a skillet over medium-high heat. Remove the chicken thighs from the bag and pat dry with paper towels. Sear the chicken thighs, skin side down, in the skillet for 3-4 minutes until the skin is crispy and golden brown.
7. Serve the chicken thighs hot with your favorite side dishes and enjoy!

Nutritional information: (per serving) 350 calories, 30g protein, 0g carbohydrates, 25g fat, 0g fiber, 150mg cholesterol, 300mg sodium, 400mg potassium

Sous Vide Chicken Wings

Yield: 4 servings | Prep time: 10 minutes | Cook time: 2 hours

Ingredients:

- 2 pounds of chicken wings
- 2 tablespoons soy sauce
- 2 tablespoons honey
- 2 cloves garlic, minced
- 1 teaspoon grated ginger
- Salt and pepper to taste
- Sesame seeds and chopped green onions for garnish (optional)

Directions:

1. Preheat the sous vide water bath to 165°F (74°C).
2. In a bowl, mix soy sauce, honey, minced garlic, grated ginger, salt, and pepper to make the marinade.
3. Place the chicken wings in a large resealable bag and pour the marinade over them. Seal the bag and massage the marinade into the wings until they are evenly coated.
4. Once the water bath has reached the desired temperature, place the sealed bag in the water bath and cook for 2 hours.
5. After 2 hours, remove the bag from the water bath and take out the chicken wings.
6. Preheat the oven broiler or grill to high heat. Transfer the chicken wings to a baking sheet lined with foil and broil or grill them for 5-7 minutes on each side until they are crispy and golden brown.
7. Serve the chicken wings hot, garnished with sesame seeds and chopped green onions if desired.

Nutritional information: (per serving) 350 calories, 25g protein, 15g carbohydrates, 20g fat, 0g fiber, 85mg cholesterol, 800mg sodium, 250mg potassium

Sous Vide Chicken Legs

Yield: 4 servings | Prep time: 10 minutes | Cook time: 2 hours

Ingredients:

- 8 chicken legs
- 2 tablespoons olive oil
- 4 cloves garlic, minced
- 2 teaspoons smoked paprika
- Salt and pepper to taste
- Chopped parsley for garnish (optional)

Directions:

1. Preheat the sous vide water bath to 165°F (74°C).
2. Season the chicken legs with salt, pepper, and smoked paprika.
3. Place the seasoned chicken legs, minced garlic, and olive oil in a vacuum-sealed bag. Remove as much air as possible and seal the bag.
4. Once the water bath has reached the desired temperature, place the sealed bag in the water bath and cook for 2 hours.
5. After 2 hours, remove the bag from the water bath and take out the chicken legs.
6. Preheat a skillet over medium-high heat. Remove the chicken legs from the bag and pat dry with paper towels. Sear the chicken legs in the skillet for 3-4 minutes on each side until they are golden brown.
7. Serve the chicken legs hot, garnished with chopped parsley if desired.

Nutritional information: (per serving) 350 calories, 30g protein, 0g carbohydrates, 25g fat, 0g fiber, 140mg cholesterol, 400mg sodium, 350mg potassium

Sous Vide Chicken Tenders

Yield: 4 servings | Prep time: 10 minutes | Cook time: 1 hour

Ingredients:

- 1 pound chicken tenders
- 2 tablespoons olive oil
- 2 teaspoons garlic powder
- 1 teaspoon paprika
- Salt and pepper to taste
- Lemon wedges for serving (optional)

Directions:

1. Preheat the sous vide water bath to 145°F (63°C).
2. In a bowl, mix olive oil, garlic powder, paprika, salt, and pepper to create a marinade.

3.   Place the chicken tenders in a resealable bag and pour the marinade over them. Seal the bag and massage the marinade into the chicken tenders until they are evenly coated.

4.   Once the water bath has reached the desired temperature, place the sealed bag in the water bath and cook for 1 hour.

5.   After 1 hour, remove the bag from the water bath and take out the chicken tenders.

6.   Preheat a skillet over medium-high heat. Remove the chicken tenders from the bag and pat dry with paper towels. Sear the chicken tenders in the skillet for 2-3 minutes on each side until they are golden brown.

7.   Serve the chicken tenders hot, with lemon wedges on the side for squeezing over the top if desired.

Nutritional information: (per serving) 250 calories, 30g protein, 0g carbohydrates, 13g fat, 0g fiber, 85mg cholesterol, 300mg sodium, 200mg potassium

Sous Vide Chicken Curry

Yield: 4 servings | Prep time: 15 minutes | Cook time: 2 hours

Ingredients:

- 1 pound boneless, skinless chicken breasts, cut into bite-sized pieces
- 2 tablespoons olive oil
- 1 onion, finely chopped
- 2 cloves garlic, minced
- 1 tablespoon ginger paste
- 2 tablespoons curry powder
- 1 teaspoon ground turmeric
- 1 teaspoon ground cumin
- 1 teaspoon ground coriander
- 1 can (14 oz) coconut milk
- Salt and pepper to taste
- Fresh cilantro for garnish (optional)
- Cooked rice or naan bread for serving

Directions:

1.   Preheat the sous vide water bath to 145°F (63°C).

2.   Season the chicken pieces with salt and pepper.

3.   Heat olive oil in a skillet over medium heat. Add the chopped onion, garlic, and ginger paste. Cook until the onion is soft and translucent, about 5 minutes.

4.   Stir in the curry powder, turmeric, cumin, and coriander. Cook for another 2 minutes until fragrant.

5.   Add the seasoned chicken pieces to the skillet and cook until browned on all sides, about 5 minutes.

6.   Transfer the chicken mixture to a vacuum-sealed bag. Pour in the coconut milk, then seal the bag.

7.   Once the water bath has reached the desired temperature, place the sealed bag in the water bath and cook for 2 hours.

8.   After 2 hours, remove the bag from the water bath and take out the chicken curry.

9.   Serve the chicken curry hot over cooked rice or with naan bread. Garnish with fresh cilantro if desired.

Nutritional information: (per serving) 380 calories, 25g protein, 10g carbohydrates, 28g fat, 2g fiber, 60mg cholesterol, 450mg sodium, 300mg potassium

Sous Vide Chicken Teriyaki

Yield: 4 servings | Prep time: 10 minutes | Cook time: 1 hour

Ingredients:

- 4 boneless, skinless chicken breasts
- 1/2 cup soy sauce
- 1/4 cup mirin (Japanese sweet rice wine)
- 2 tablespoons honey
- 2 cloves garlic, minced
- 1 teaspoon grated ginger
- 1 tablespoon sesame oil
- 2 green onions, chopped (for garnish)
- Sesame seeds (for garnish)
- Cooked rice, for serving

Directions:

1.	Preheat the sous vide water bath to 145°F (63°C).
2.	In a bowl, whisk together soy sauce, mirin, honey, minced garlic, grated ginger, and sesame oil to make the teriyaki sauce.
3.	Place the chicken breasts in a vacuum-sealed bag and pour the teriyaki sauce over them. Seal the bag and massage the sauce into the chicken breasts until evenly coated.
4.	Once the water bath has reached the desired temperature, place the sealed bag in the water bath and cook for 1 hour.
5.	After 1 hour, remove the bag from the water bath and take out the chicken breasts.
6.	Preheat a skillet over medium-high heat. Remove the chicken breasts from the bag and pat dry with paper towels. Sear the chicken breasts in the skillet for 2-3 minutes on each side until they are golden brown and caramelized.
7.	Slice the chicken breasts and serve over cooked rice. Garnish with chopped green onions and sesame seeds.

Nutritional information: (per serving) 300 calories, 30g protein, 15g carbohydrates, 10g fat, 1g fiber, 70mg cholesterol, 1000mg sodium, 250mg potassium

Sous Vide Chicken Soup

Yield: 4 servings | Prep time: 15 minutes | Cook time: 2 hours

Ingredients:

- 2 boneless, skinless chicken breasts

- 4 cups chicken broth
- 2 carrots, peeled and sliced
- 2 celery stalks, sliced
- 1 onion, chopped
- 2 cloves garlic, minced
- 1 teaspoon dried thyme
- Salt and pepper to taste
- Fresh parsley for garnish (optional)

Directions:

1. Preheat the sous vide water bath to 145°F (63°C).
2. Place the chicken breasts, chicken broth, carrots, celery, onion, garlic, and dried thyme in a large resealable bag.
3. Remove as much air as possible from the bag and seal it tightly.
4. Once the water bath has reached the desired temperature, place the sealed bag in the water bath and cook for 2 hours.
5. After 2 hours, remove the bag from the water bath and take out the chicken breasts.
6. Shred the chicken breasts using two forks and return the shredded chicken to the soup.
7. Season the soup with salt and pepper to taste.
8. Serve the chicken soup hot, garnished with fresh parsley if desired.

Nutritional information: (per serving) 150 calories, 20g protein, 10g carbohydrates, 2g fat, 2g fiber, 40mg cholesterol, 800mg sodium, 500mg potassium

Sous Vide Chicken Salad

Yield: 4 servings | Prep time: 15 minutes | Cook time: 1 hour

Ingredients:

- 2 boneless, skinless chicken breasts
- 4 cups mixed salad greens
- 1 cucumber, sliced
- 1 bell pepper, sliced
- 1 cup cherry tomatoes, halved
- 1/4 cup sliced red onion
- 1/4 cup crumbled feta cheese (optional)
- 1/4 cup sliced almonds (optional)
- Your favorite salad dressing

Directions:

1. Preheat the sous vide water bath to 145°F (63°C).
2. Season the chicken breasts with salt and pepper.
3. Place the chicken breasts in a vacuum-sealed bag and remove as much air as possible.

4.   Once the water bath has reached the desired temperature, place the sealed bag in the water bath and cook for 1 hour.

5.   After 1 hour, remove the bag from the water bath and take out the chicken breasts.

6.   Preheat a skillet over medium-high heat. Remove the chicken breasts from the bag and pat dry with paper towels. Sear the chicken breasts in the skillet for 2-3 minutes on each side until they are golden brown and cooked through.

7.   Let the chicken breasts rest for a few minutes, then slice them thinly.

8.   In a large bowl, combine the mixed salad greens, cucumber, bell pepper, cherry tomatoes, and sliced red onion. Top the salad with the sliced chicken breasts. If desired, sprinkle crumbled feta cheese and sliced almonds over the salad.

9.   Drizzle your favorite salad dressing over the salad and toss to coat evenly.

10.   Serve the chicken salad immediately.

Nutritional information: (per serving) 250 calories, 25g protein, 10g carbohydrates, 10g fat, 4g fiber, 60mg cholesterol, 300mg sodium, 400mg potassium

Sous Vide Chicken Fajitas

Yield: 4 servings | Prep time: 15 minutes | Cook time: 1 hour

Ingredients:

- 1 pound boneless, skinless chicken breasts
- 1 tablespoon olive oil
- 1 bell pepper, thinly sliced
- 1 onion, thinly sliced
- 2 cloves garlic, minced
- 1 tablespoon chili powder
- 1 teaspoon ground cumin
- 1 teaspoon smoked paprika
- Salt and pepper to taste
- Flour tortillas, for serving
- Optional toppings: salsa, guacamole, sour cream, shredded cheese, chopped cilantro

Directions:

1.   Preheat the sous vide water bath to 145°F (63°C).

2.   Season the chicken breasts with salt, pepper, chili powder, ground cumin, and smoked paprika.

3.   Place the seasoned chicken breasts in a vacuum-sealed bag along with the sliced bell pepper, sliced onion, minced garlic, and olive oil. Remove as much air as possible and seal the bag.

4.   Once the water bath has reached the desired temperature, place the sealed bag in the water bath and cook for 1 hour.

5.   After 1 hour, remove the bag from the water bath and take out the chicken breasts.

6.   Preheat a skillet over medium-high heat. Remove the chicken breasts from the bag and pat dry with paper towels. Sear the chicken breasts in the skillet for 2-3 minutes on each side until they are golden brown and cooked through.

7.   While the chicken is searing, heat another skillet over medium heat. Add the sliced bell pepper and onion from the bag and cook until they are tender about 5-7 minutes.

8.   Slice the cooked chicken breasts thinly.

9.   Serve the sliced chicken, bell peppers, and onions on warm flour tortillas. Top with your favorite toppings such as salsa, guacamole, sour cream, shredded cheese, and chopped cilantro.

10.   Roll up the tortillas and enjoy your delicious chicken fajitas!

Nutritional information: (per serving) 300 calories, 25g protein, 30g carbohydrates, 10g fat, 5g fiber, 60mg cholesterol, 400mg sodium, 500mg potassium

Turkey

Sous Vide Turkey Breast

Yield: 4 servings | Prep time: 10 minutes | Cook time: 3 hours

Ingredients:

- 2 pounds boneless, skinless turkey breast
- 2 tablespoons olive oil
- 2 cloves garlic, minced
- 1 tablespoon chopped fresh thyme (or 1 teaspoon dried thyme)
- 1 tablespoon chopped fresh rosemary (or 1 teaspoon dried rosemary)
- Salt and pepper to taste

Directions:

1.   Preheat the sous vide water bath to 145°F (63°C).

2.   Season the turkey breast with salt, pepper, minced garlic, chopped thyme, and chopped rosemary.

3.   Place the seasoned turkey breast in a vacuum-sealed bag along with olive oil. Remove as much air as possible and seal the bag.

4.   Once the water bath has reached the desired temperature, place the sealed bag in the water bath and cook for 3 hours.

5.   After 3 hours, remove the bag from the water bath and take out the turkey breast.

6.   Preheat a skillet over medium-high heat. Remove the turkey breast from the bag and pat dry with paper towels. Sear the turkey breast in the skillet for 2-3 minutes on each side until it is golden brown.

7.   Let the turkey breast rest for a few minutes before slicing it thinly.

8.   Serve the sliced turkey breast hot with your favorite side dishes.

Nutritional information: (per serving) 200 calories, 40g protein, 0g carbohydrates, 5g fat, 0g fiber, 100mg cholesterol, 200mg sodium, 400mg potassium

Sous Vide Turkey Legs

Yield: 4 servings | Prep time: 10 minutes | Cook time: 8 hours

Ingredients:

- 4 turkey legs
- 2 tablespoons olive oil

- 4 cloves garlic, minced
- 1 tablespoon chopped fresh sage (or 1 teaspoon dried sage)
- 1 tablespoon chopped fresh thyme (or 1 teaspoon dried thyme)
- Salt and pepper to taste

Directions:

1. Preheat the sous vide water bath to 165°F (74°C).
2. Season the turkey legs with salt, pepper, minced garlic, chopped sage, and chopped thyme.
3. Place the seasoned turkey legs in a vacuum-sealed bag along with olive oil. Remove as much air as possible and seal the bag.
4. Once the water bath has reached the desired temperature, place the sealed bag in the water bath and cook for 8 hours.
5. After 8 hours, remove the bag from the water bath and take out the turkey legs.
6. Preheat a grill or a cast-iron skillet over medium-high heat.
7. Remove the turkey legs from the bag and pat dry with paper towels. Sear the turkey legs on the grill or in the skillet for 3-4 minutes on each side until they are golden brown and crispy.
8. Serve the turkey legs hot with your favorite side dishes.

Nutritional information: (per serving) 400 calories, 40g protein, 0g carbohydrates, 25g fat, 0g fiber, 200mg cholesterol, 300mg sodium, 500mg potassium

Sous Vide Turkey Thighs

Yield: 4 servings | Prep time: 10 minutes | Cook time: 4 hours
Ingredients:

- 4 turkey thighs
- 2 tablespoons olive oil
- 4 cloves garlic, minced
- 1 tablespoon chopped fresh rosemary (or 1 teaspoon dried rosemary)
- 1 tablespoon chopped fresh thyme (or 1 teaspoon dried thyme)
- Salt and pepper to taste

Directions:
1. Preheat the sous vide water bath to 165°F (74°C).
2. Season the turkey thighs with salt, pepper, minced garlic, chopped rosemary, and chopped thyme.
3. Place the seasoned turkey thighs in a vacuum-sealed bag along with olive oil. Remove as much air as possible and seal the bag.
4. Once the water bath has reached the desired temperature, place the sealed bag in the water bath and cook for 4 hours.
5. After 4 hours, remove the bag from the water bath and take out the turkey thighs.
6. Preheat a skillet over medium-high heat. Remove the turkey thighs from the bag and pat dry with paper towels. Sear the turkey thighs in the skillet for 3-4 minutes on each side until they are golden brown and crispy.
7. Serve the turkey thighs hot with your favorite side dishes.
Nutritional information: (per serving) 350 calories, 40g protein, 0g carbohydrates, 20g fat, 0g fiber, 200mg cholesterol, 300mg sodium, 450mg potassium

Sous Vide Turkey Wings

Yield: 4 servings | Prep time: 10 minutes | Cook time: 8 hours
Ingredients:

- 4 turkey wings
- 2 tablespoons olive oil
- 4 cloves garlic, minced
- 1 tablespoon chopped fresh thyme (or 1 teaspoon dried thyme)
- 1 tablespoon chopped fresh rosemary (or 1 teaspoon dried rosemary)
- Salt and pepper to taste

Directions:

1. Preheat the sous vide water bath to 165°F (74°C).
2. Season the turkey wings with salt, pepper, minced garlic, chopped thyme, and chopped rosemary.
3. Place the seasoned turkey wings in a vacuum-sealed bag along with olive oil. Remove as much air as possible and seal the bag.
4. Once the water bath has reached the desired temperature, place the sealed bag in the water bath and cook for 8 hours.
5. After 8 hours, remove the bag from the water bath and take out the turkey wings.
6. Preheat a grill or a cast-iron skillet over medium-high heat.
7. Remove the turkey wings from the bag and pat dry with paper towels. Sear the turkey wings on the grill or in the skillet for 3-4 minutes on each side until they are golden brown and crispy.
8. Serve the turkey wings hot with your favorite side dishes.

Nutritional information: (per serving) 400 calories, 30g protein, 0g carbohydrates, 30g fat, 0g fiber, 200mg cholesterol, 300mg sodium, 450mg potassium

Sous Vide Turkey Roulade

Yield: 4 servings | Prep time: 20 minutes | Cook time: 2 hours

Ingredients:

- 1 boneless turkey breast, butterflied (about 2 pounds)
- 4 slices of prosciutto
- 1 cup baby spinach leaves
- 1/2 cup shredded mozzarella cheese
- 2 tablespoons olive oil
- 2 cloves garlic, minced
- 1 tablespoon chopped fresh sage (or 1 teaspoon dried sage)
- Salt and pepper to taste

Directions:

1. Preheat the sous vide water bath to 145°F (63°C).
2. Lay the butterflied turkey breast flat on a cutting board. Season both sides with salt, pepper, minced garlic, and chopped sage.
3. Layer the prosciutto slices over the turkey breast, covering the entire surface.
4. Spread the baby spinach leaves evenly over the prosciutto.
5. Sprinkle the shredded mozzarella cheese over the spinach leaves.
6. Starting from one end, tightly roll up the turkey breast into a roulade.
7. Secure the roulade with kitchen twine, tying it at regular intervals.
8. Place the roulade in a vacuum-sealed bag along with olive oil. Remove as much air as possible and seal the bag.
9. Once the water bath has reached the desired temperature, place the sealed bag in the water bath and cook for 2 hours.
10. After 2 hours, remove the bag from the water bath and take out the turkey roulade.

11. Preheat a skillet over medium-high heat. Remove the turkey roulade from the bag and pat dry with paper towels. Sear the roulade in the skillet for 2-3 minutes on each side until it is golden brown.
12. Let the turkey roulade rest for a few minutes before slicing it into rounds.
13. Serve the sliced turkey roulade hot with your favorite side dishes.

Nutritional information: (per serving) 300 calories, 40g protein, 2g carbohydrates, 15g fat, 1g fiber, 100mg cholesterol, 400mg sodium, 500mg potassium

Sous Vide Turkey Breast Roast

Yield: 4 servings | Prep time: 15 minutes | Cook time: 3 hours
Ingredients:

- 1 boneless turkey breast (about 2 pounds)
- 2 tablespoons olive oil
- 2 cloves garlic, minced
- 1 tablespoon chopped fresh thyme (or 1 teaspoon dried thyme)
- 1 tablespoon chopped fresh rosemary (or 1 teaspoon dried rosemary)
- Salt and pepper to taste

Directions:

1. Preheat the sous vide water bath to 145°F (63°C).
2. Season the turkey breast with salt, pepper, minced garlic, chopped thyme, and chopped rosemary.
3. Place the seasoned turkey breast in a vacuum-sealed bag along with olive oil. Remove as much air as possible and seal the bag.
4. Once the water bath has reached the desired temperature, place the sealed bag in the water bath and cook for 3 hours.
5. After 3 hours, remove the bag from the water bath and take out the turkey breast.
6. Preheat the oven to 425°F (220°C).
7. Remove the turkey breast from the bag and pat dry with paper towels. Transfer it to a roasting pan.
8. Roast the turkey breast in the preheated oven for 15-20 minutes, or until the skin is golden brown and crispy.
9. Let the turkey breast rest for a few minutes before slicing it thinly.
10. Serve the sliced turkey breast roast hot with your favorite side dishes.

Nutritional information: (per serving) 250 calories, 40g protein, 0g carbohydrates, 10g fat, 0g fiber, 100mg cholesterol, 300mg sodium, 500mg potassium

Sous Vide Turkey Meatballs

Yield: 4 servings | Prep time: 15 minutes | Cook time: 1 hour
Ingredients:

- 1 pound ground turkey
- 1/4 cup breadcrumbs
- 1/4 cup grated Parmesan cheese
- 1/4 cup chopped fresh parsley
- 1 egg
- 2 cloves garlic, minced
- Salt and pepper to taste

Directions:

1. Preheat the sous vide water bath to 145°F (63°C).
2. In a mixing bowl, combine ground turkey, breadcrumbs, Parmesan cheese, parsley, egg, garlic, salt, and pepper. Mix until well combined.
3. Form the mixture into meatballs, about 1 inch in diameter.
4. Place the meatballs in a single layer in a vacuum-sealed bag or a ziplock bag, ensuring they are not crowded.
5. Seal the bag using a vacuum sealer or the water displacement method.
6. Place the sealed bag in the preheated water bath and cook for 1 hour.
7. Once cooked, remove the bag from the water bath, carefully open it, and transfer the meatballs to a serving plate.

Nutritional information: Approx. 240 calories, 32g protein, 8g carbohydrates, 9g fat, 1g fiber, 180mg cholesterol, 380mg sodium, 380mg potassium

Sous Vide Turkey Chili

Yield: 4 servings | Prep time: 15 minutes | Cook time: 2 hours
Ingredients:

- 1 pound ground turkey
- 1 onion, diced
- 1 bell pepper, diced
- 2 cloves garlic, minced
- 1 can (15 ounces) kidney beans, drained and rinsed
- 1 can (15 ounces) diced tomatoes
- 1 cup chicken broth
- 2 tablespoons chili powder
- 1 teaspoon ground cumin
- Salt and pepper to taste
- Optional toppings: shredded cheese, sour cream, chopped cilantro

Directions:

1. Preheat the sous vide water bath to 155°F (68°C).
2. In a skillet, cook the ground turkey until browned, breaking it apart with a spoon. Drain excess fat and transfer the turkey to a sous vide bag.
3. Add diced onion, bell pepper, minced garlic, kidney beans, diced tomatoes, chicken broth, chili powder, cumin, salt, and pepper to the bag with the turkey.
4. Seal the bag using a vacuum sealer or the water displacement method.
5. Place the sealed bag in the preheated water bath and cook for 2 hours.
6. Once cooked, carefully open the bag and transfer the chili to serving bowls.
7. Serve hot with optional toppings if desired.

Nutritional information: Approx. 280 calories, 26g protein, 25g carbohydrates, 8g fat, 7g fiber, 65mg cholesterol, 680mg sodium, 800mg potassium

Sous Vide Turkey Soup

Yield: 4 servings | Prep time: 15 minutes | Cook time: 3 hours
Ingredients:

- 1 pound turkey breast, diced
- 4 cups chicken or turkey broth

- 1 onion, chopped
- 2 carrots, sliced
- 2 celery stalks, sliced
- 2 cloves garlic, minced
- 1 teaspoon dried thyme
- 1 teaspoon dried sage
- Salt and pepper to taste
- Optional garnish: chopped parsley

Directions:

1. Preheat the sous vide water bath to 150°F (65°C).
2. Season the diced turkey breast with salt and pepper and place it in a sous vide bag along with chopped onion, sliced carrots, sliced celery, minced garlic, dried thyme, and dried sage.
3. Pour the chicken or turkey broth into the bag, ensuring all ingredients are submerged.
4. Seal the bag using a vacuum sealer or the water displacement method.
5. Place the sealed bag in the preheated water bath and cook for 3 hours.
6. Once cooked, carefully open the bag and transfer the soup to serving bowls.
7. Garnish with chopped parsley if desired before serving.

Nutritional information: Approx. 180 calories, 25g protein, 10g carbohydrates, 4g fat, 2g fiber, 55mg cholesterol, 980mg sodium, 480mg potassium

Sous Vide Turkey Carnitas

Yield: 4 servings | Prep time: 15 minutes | Cook time: 8 hours
Ingredients:

- 1 pound turkey thighs, boneless and skinless
- 2 cloves garlic, minced
- 1 teaspoon ground cumin
- 1 teaspoon chili powder
- 1 teaspoon dried oregano
- 1 teaspoon paprika
- 1/2 teaspoon ground coriander
- Salt and pepper to taste
- 1 tablespoon olive oil
- Juice of 1 lime
- Corn tortillas, for serving
- Optional toppings: diced onion, chopped cilantro, salsa, lime wedges

Directions:

1. Preheat the sous vide water bath to 165°F (74°C).
2. In a bowl, mix minced garlic, ground cumin, chili powder, dried oregano, paprika, ground coriander, salt, pepper, olive oil, and lime juice to make a marinade.
3. Pat dry the turkey thighs and rub them with the marinade mixture.
4. Place the turkey thighs in a sous vide bag, ensuring they are in a single layer.
5. Seal the bag using a vacuum sealer or the water displacement method.
6. Place the sealed bag in the preheated water bath and cook for 8 hours.
7. Once cooked, remove the turkey thighs from the bag and shred them using two forks.
8. Heat a skillet over medium-high heat and sear the shredded turkey for a few minutes until crispy.

9. Serve the turkey carnitas in corn tortillas with optional toppings.

Nutritional information: Approx. 240 calories, 25g protein, 4g carbohydrates, 14g fat, 1g fiber, 90mg cholesterol, 380mg sodium, 300mg potassium

Duck

Sous Vide Duck Breast with Orange Sauce

Yield: 4 servings | Prep time: 15 minutes | Cook time: 1 hour 30 minutes

Ingredients:

- 2 duck breasts
- Salt and pepper to taste
- 1 tablespoon olive oil
- 1/2 cup orange juice
- Zest of 1 orange
- 2 tablespoons honey
- 2 cloves garlic, minced
- 1 tablespoon soy sauce
- 1 teaspoon cornstarch (optional, for thickening)

Directions:

1. Preheat the sous vide water bath to 135°F (57°C).
2. Season the duck breasts with salt and pepper on both sides.
3. Place the duck breasts in separate sous vide bags, drizzle with olive oil, and seal the bags using a vacuum sealer or the water displacement method.
4. Place the sealed bags in the preheated water bath and cook for 1 hour 30 minutes.
5. While the duck is cooking, prepare the orange sauce. In a saucepan, combine orange juice, orange zest, honey, minced garlic, and soy sauce. Bring to a simmer over medium heat and let it cook for 5-7 minutes until slightly thickened. If desired, mix cornstarch with a little water and add to the sauce to thicken further. Remove from heat and set aside.
6. Once the duck is cooked, remove it from the sous vide bags and pat dry with paper towels.
7. Heat a skillet over medium-high heat. Sear the duck breasts, skin side down, for 3-4 minutes until the skin is crispy. Flip and sear the other side for an additional 2-3 minutes.
8. Let the duck rest for a few minutes before slicing.
9. Serve the sliced duck breast with the orange sauce drizzled over the top.

Nutritional information: Approx. 300 calories, 25g protein, 10g carbohydrates, 18g fat, 0.5g fiber, 90mg cholesterol, 300mg sodium, 280mg potassium

Sous Vide Duck Leg Tacos

Yield: 4 servings | Prep time: 15 minutes | Cook time: 8 hours

Ingredients:

- 4 duck legs

- Salt and pepper to taste
- 1 tablespoon olive oil
- 1 teaspoon ground cumin
- 1 teaspoon smoked paprika
- 1 teaspoon garlic powder
- 1 teaspoon onion powder
- 1/2 teaspoon chili powder
- 8 small corn tortillas
- Optional toppings: chopped onion, chopped cilantro, sliced radishes, lime wedges

Directions:

1. Preheat the sous vide water bath to 165°F (74°C).
2. Season the duck legs with salt, pepper, ground cumin, smoked paprika, garlic powder, onion powder, and chili powder.
3. Place each duck leg in a separate sous vide bag, drizzle with olive oil, and seal the bags using a vacuum sealer or the water displacement method.
4. Place the sealed bags in the preheated water bath and cook for 8 hours.
5. Once cooked, remove the duck legs from the sous vide bags and pat dry with paper towels.
6. Heat a skillet over medium-high heat. Sear the duck legs, skin side down, for 3-4 minutes until the skin is crispy. Flip and sear the other side for an additional 2-3 minutes.
7. Remove the duck meat from the bones and shred it using two forks.
8. Warm the corn tortillas in the skillet or microwave.
9. Fill each tortilla with shredded duck meat and desired toppings.
10. Serve the duck leg tacos hot with lime wedges on the side.

Nutritional information: Approx. 300 calories, 20g protein, 20g carbohydrates, 15g fat, 2g fiber, 80mg cholesterol, 300mg sodium, 200mg potassium

Duck Delight Sous Vide

Yield: 2 servings | Prep time: 10 minutes | Cook time: 2 hours

Ingredients:

- 2 duck breasts
- Salt and pepper to taste
- 1 tablespoon olive oil
- 1 cup red wine
- 2 tablespoons balsamic vinegar
- 2 tablespoons honey
- 2 cloves garlic, minced
- 1 sprig of fresh thyme
- 1 tablespoon butter (optional)

Directions:

1. Preheat the sous vide water bath to 135°F (57°C).
2. Season the duck breasts generously with salt and pepper.
3. Place the duck breasts in a vacuum-sealed bag or a zip-top bag, ensuring they are in a single layer.
4. Add olive oil to the bag and seal it, removing as much air as possible.
5. Cook the duck breasts in the sous vide water bath for 2 hours.

6. While the duck is cooking, prepare the red wine reduction. In a saucepan, combine the red wine, balsamic vinegar, honey, garlic, and thyme. Bring to a simmer over medium heat and let it reduce by half, about 15-20 minutes. Remove the thyme sprig.
7. Once the duck breasts are done cooking, remove them from the sous vide bath and pat them dry with paper towels.
8. Heat a skillet over medium-high heat and sear the duck breasts, skin-side down, for 2-3 minutes until the skin is crispy. Flip and sear for an additional 1-2 minutes.
9. Remove the duck breasts from the skillet and let them rest for a few minutes before slicing.
10. Serve the sliced duck breasts with the red wine reduction sauce drizzled over the top. Optionally, stir in butter to the sauce for added richness.

Nutritional information: (per serving) 420 calories, 25g protein, 12g carbohydrates, 28g fat, 0g fiber, 115mg cholesterol, 85mg sodium, 370mg potassium

Sous Vide Duck Leg Ramen

Yield: 4 servings | Prep time: 15 minutes | Cook time: 6 hours

Ingredients:

- 4 duck legs
- Salt and pepper to taste
- 4 cups chicken or duck broth
- 2 tablespoons soy sauce
- 1 tablespoon mirin
- 1 tablespoon sesame oil
- 1 tablespoon grated ginger
- 2 garlic cloves, minced
- 2 packs of ramen noodles
- 4 soft-boiled eggs
- 4 green onions, thinly sliced
- 2 cups baby spinach
- 1 tablespoon toasted sesame seeds (optional)
- Sriracha or chili oil for serving (optional)

Directions:

1. Preheat the sous vide water bath to 165°F (74°C).
2. Season the duck legs generously with salt and pepper.
3. Place the duck legs in a vacuum-sealed bag or a zip-top bag, ensuring they are in a single layer.
4. Add the chicken or duck broth, soy sauce, mirin, sesame oil, grated ginger, and minced garlic to the bag with the duck legs.
5. Seal the bag, removing as much air as possible, and cook in the sous vide water bath for 6 hours.
6. About 30 minutes before the duck is done cooking, prepare the ramen noodles according to the package instructions. Drain and set aside.
7. Once the duck legs are done cooking, remove them from the sous vide bath and shred the meat using two forks.
8. Divide the cooked noodles among serving bowls and top with shredded duck meat.
9. Ladle the hot broth over the noodles and duck meat.
10. Garnish each bowl with a soft-boiled egg, sliced green onions, baby spinach, and toasted sesame seeds if desired.
11. Serve immediately with sriracha or chili oil on the side for extra heat.

Nutritional information: (per serving) 550 calories, 30g protein, 30g carbohydrates, 35g fat, 3g fiber, 280mg cholesterol, 1200mg sodium, 400mg potassium

Sous Vide Duck Leg Confit

Yield: 4 servings | Prep time: 15 minutes | Cook time: 12 hours

Ingredients:

- 4 duck legs
- Salt and pepper to taste
- 4 cloves garlic, crushed
- 4 sprigs of fresh thyme
- 4 bay leaves
- 2 cups duck fat (or enough to fully submerge the duck legs)
- 1 tablespoon olive oil (optional, for searing)

Directions:

1. Preheat the sous vide water bath to 167°F (75°C).
2. Season the duck legs generously with salt and pepper.
3. Divide the crushed garlic, fresh thyme, and bay leaves evenly among the duck legs, placing them on top of each leg.
4. Place the seasoned duck legs in vacuum-sealed bags or zip-top bags, ensuring they are in a single layer.
5. Add duck fat to the bags, making sure the duck legs are fully submerged.
6. Seal the bags, remove as much air as possible, and cook in the sous vide water bath for 12 hours.
7. Once the duck legs are done cooking, carefully remove them from the bags and pat them dry with paper towels.
8. If desired, heat a skillet over medium-high heat and add olive oil. Sear the duck legs, skin-side down, for 2-3 minutes until the skin is crispy.
9. Serve the duck legs hot, either as is or alongside your favorite side dishes.

Nutritional information: (per serving) 750 calories, 30g protein, 0g carbohydrates, 70g fat, 0g fiber, 250mg cholesterol, 80mg sodium, 200mg potassium

Quail

Sous Vide Quail with Mushroom Risotto

Yield: 4 servings | Prep time: 20 minutes | Cook time: 2 hours

Ingredients: For the Sous Vide Quail:

- 4 quails, cleaned and trimmed
- Salt and pepper to taste
- 2 tablespoons olive oil
- 2 cloves garlic, minced
- 2 sprigs of fresh thyme

For the Mushroom Risotto:

- 1 cup Arborio rice

- 4 cups chicken or vegetable broth
- 2 tablespoons butter
- 1 tablespoon olive oil
- 1 shallot, finely chopped
- 2 cloves garlic, minced
- 8 ounces mushrooms (such as cremini or shiitake), sliced
- 1/2 cup dry white wine
- 1/2 cup grated Parmesan cheese
- Salt and pepper to taste
- Fresh parsley, chopped, for garnish

Directions:

1. Preheat the sous vide water bath to 145°F (63°C) for the quail.
2. Season the quail generously with salt and pepper.
3. Place the quail in vacuum-sealed bags or zip-top bags, dividing the minced garlic and thyme sprigs among them. Drizzle with olive oil, seal the bags, and ensure they are in a single layer.
4. Cook the quail in the sous vide water bath for 2 hours.
5. While the quail is cooking, prepare the mushroom risotto. In a saucepan, heat the chicken or vegetable broth until simmering, then reduce the heat to keep it warm.
6. In a separate large skillet or saucepan, heat the butter and olive oil over medium heat. Add the chopped shallot and garlic, and sauté until softened, about 2-3 minutes.
7. Add the sliced mushrooms to the skillet and cook until they release their moisture and become golden brown, about 5-6 minutes.
8. Stir in the Arborio rice and cook for 1-2 minutes until the grains are coated with oil and slightly translucent.
9. Pour in the white wine and cook, stirring constantly, until it is absorbed by the rice.
10. Begin adding the warm broth to the rice mixture, one ladleful at a time, stirring frequently and allowing each addition to be absorbed before adding more. Continue this process until the rice is creamy and cooked to your desired consistency, about 18-20 minutes.
11. Once the quail is done cooking, remove them from the sous vide bath and pat them dry with paper towels.
12. Heat a skillet over high heat and sear the quail for 1-2 minutes on each side until golden brown and crispy.
13. Serve the sous vide quail hot alongside the mushroom risotto, garnished with grated Parmesan cheese and chopped parsley.

Nutritional information: (per serving) 550 calories, 25g protein, 45g carbohydrates, 28g fat, 4g fiber, 80mg cholesterol, 900mg sodium, 400mg potassium

Sous Vide Quail with Bacon

Yield: 4 servings | Prep time: 15 minutes | Cook time: 2 hours

Ingredients:

- 4 quails, cleaned and trimmed
- Salt and pepper to taste
- 8 slices of bacon

- 2 tablespoons olive oil
- 2 cloves garlic, minced
- 2 sprigs of fresh thyme
- 1 tablespoon chopped fresh parsley, for garnish

Directions:

1. Preheat the sous vide water bath to 145°F (63°C).
2. Season the quails generously with salt and pepper.
3. Wrap each quail with 2 slices of bacon, securing them with kitchen twine if necessary.
4. Place the bacon-wrapped quails in vacuum-sealed bags or zip-top bags, dividing the minced garlic and thyme sprigs among them. Drizzle with olive oil, seal the bags, and ensure they are in a single layer.
5. Cook the quails in the sous vide water bath for 2 hours.
6. Once the quails are done cooking, remove them from the bags and pat them dry with paper towels.
7. Heat a skillet over medium-high heat and sear the quails, bacon-side down, for 2-3 minutes until the bacon is crispy. Flip and sear for an additional 1-2 minutes on the other side.
8. Serve the sous vide quails hot, garnished with chopped fresh parsley.

Nutritional information: (per serving) 400 calories, 30g protein, 2g carbohydrates, 30g fat, 0g fiber, 100mg cholesterol, 500mg sodium, 250mg potassium

Sous Vide Stuffed Quail

Yield: 4 servings | Prep time: 25 minutes | Cook time: 2 hours

Ingredients:

- 4 quails, cleaned and trimmed
- Salt and pepper to taste
- 8 slices prosciutto or bacon
- 1/2 cup breadcrumbs
- 1/4 cup grated Parmesan cheese
- 2 cloves garlic, minced
- 2 tablespoons chopped fresh parsley
- Zest of 1 lemon
- 2 tablespoons olive oil
- 2 sprigs of fresh thyme
- 2 tablespoons butter
- 1 tablespoon olive oil
- Salt and pepper to taste
- Chopped fresh parsley, for garnish

Directions:

1. Preheat the sous vide water bath to 145°F (63°C).
2. In a bowl, combine breadcrumbs, Parmesan cheese, minced garlic, chopped parsley, lemon zest, and olive oil. Mix until well combined.

3. Season the quails inside and out with salt and pepper.
4. Stuff each quail with the breadcrumb mixture and wrap each stuffed quail with 2 slices of prosciutto or bacon, securing them with kitchen twine if necessary.
5. Place the stuffed and wrapped quails in vacuum-sealed bags or zip-top bags, dividing the fresh thyme sprigs among them. Seal the bags, removing as much air as possible, and ensure they are in a single layer.
6. Cook the stuffed quails in the sous vide water bath for 2 hours.
7. Once the quails are done cooking, remove them from the bags and pat them dry with paper towels.
8. Heat a skillet over medium-high heat and add butter and olive oil. Sear the quails, turning occasionally, until the prosciutto or bacon is crispy and the quails are golden brown on all sides, about 5-6 minutes.
9. Serve the sous vide stuffed quails hot, garnished with chopped fresh parsley.

Nutritional information: (per serving) 450 calories, 30g protein, 10g carbohydrates, 30g fat, 1g fiber, 100mg cholesterol, 600mg sodium, 200mg potassium

Dove

Sous Vide Dove Poppers

Yield: 4 servings | Prep time: 20 minutes | Cook time: 2 hours

Ingredients:

- 8 dove breasts
- Salt and pepper to taste
- 8 slices jalapeno peppers, halved lengthwise
- 4 slices bacon, cut into halves widthwise
- 1/4 cup cream cheese, softened
- 1 tablespoon olive oil

Directions:

1. Preheat the sous vide water bath to 135°F (57°C).
2. Season the dove breasts with salt and pepper.
3. Place a slice of jalapeno on top of each dove breast, then wrap each piece with a half-slice of bacon, securing it with a toothpick.
4. Place the wrapped dove breasts in vacuum-sealed bags or zip-top bags, ensuring they are in a single layer.
5. Add olive oil to the bags, and seal them, removing as much air as possible.
6. Cook the dove poppers in the sous vide water bath for 2 hours.
7. Once the dove poppers are done cooking, remove them from the bags and pat them dry with paper towels.
8. Preheat a grill or grill pan to medium-high heat.
9. Grill the dove poppers for 2-3 minutes on each side, or until the bacon is crispy and the dove breasts are cooked through.
10. Serve the sous vide dove poppers hot, optionally with a side of dipping sauce or salsa.

Nutritional information: (per serving) 250 calories, 25g protein, 2g carbohydrates, 15g fat, 0g fiber, 70mg cholesterol, 400mg sodium, 200mg potassium

Sous Vide Dove Stew

Yield: 4 servings | Prep time: 15 minutes | Cook time: 4 hours

Ingredients:

- 8 dove breasts
- Salt and pepper to taste
- 2 tablespoons olive oil
- 1 onion, chopped
- 2 cloves garlic, minced
- 2 carrots, peeled and chopped
- 2 celery stalks, chopped
- 1 cup diced tomatoes
- 4 cups chicken or vegetable broth
- 2 bay leaves
- 1 teaspoon dried thyme
- 1 teaspoon dried rosemary
- 1 teaspoon paprika
- Salt and pepper to taste
- Chopped fresh parsley, for garnish

Directions:

1. Preheat the sous vide water bath to 155°F (68°C).
2. Season the dove breasts with salt and pepper.
3. Place the dove breasts in vacuum-sealed bags or zip-top bags, ensuring they are in a single layer.
4. Add olive oil to the bags, and seal them, removing as much air as possible.
5. Cook the dove breasts in the sous vide water bath for 4 hours.
6. Once the dove breasts are done cooking, remove them from the bags and pat them dry with paper towels. Reserve the cooking juices.
7. In a large pot or Dutch oven, heat a tablespoon of olive oil over medium heat. Add the chopped onion and cook until softened about 5 minutes.
8. Add the minced garlic, chopped carrots, and chopped celery to the pot. Cook for another 5 minutes, stirring occasionally.
9. Stir in the diced tomatoes, chicken or vegetable broth, bay leaves, dried thyme, dried rosemary, paprika, reserved cooking juices from the sous vide bags, and season with salt and pepper to taste.
10. Bring the stew to a simmer, then reduce the heat to low and let it simmer for 30-40 minutes, allowing the flavors to meld together.
11. Remove the bay leaves from the stew and discard them.
12. Add the sous vide dove breasts to the stew and let them heat through for a few minutes.
13. Serve the sous vide dove stew hot, garnished with chopped fresh parsley.

Nutritional information: (per serving) 300 calories, 30g protein, 10g carbohydrates, 15g fat, 2g fiber, 70mg cholesterol, 800mg sodium, 400mg potassium

Sous Vide Dove Curry

Yield: 4 servings | Prep time: 20 minutes | Cook time: 2 hours

Ingredients:

- 8 dove breasts
- Salt and pepper to taste
- 2 tablespoons olive oil
- 1 onion, finely chopped
- 2 cloves garlic, minced
- 1 tablespoon ginger, minced
- 2 tablespoons curry powder
- 1 can (14 oz) coconut milk
- 1 cup chicken or vegetable broth
- 2 cups diced tomatoes
- 2 potatoes, peeled and diced
- 1 cup green peas (fresh or frozen)
- Salt and pepper to taste
- Chopped fresh cilantro, for garnish
- Cooked rice or naan bread, for serving

Directions:

1. Preheat the sous vide water bath to 155°F (68°C).
2. Season the dove breasts with salt and pepper.
3. Place the dove breasts in vacuum-sealed bags or zip-top bags, ensuring they are in a single layer.
4. Add olive oil to the bags, and seal them, removing as much air as possible.
5. Cook the dove breasts in the sous vide water bath for 2 hours.
6. Once the dove breasts are done cooking, remove them from the bags and pat them dry with paper towels.
7. In a large skillet or saucepan, heat a tablespoon of olive oil over medium heat. Add the chopped onion and cook until softened about 5 minutes.
8. Add the minced garlic, minced ginger, and curry powder to the skillet. Cook for another 2 minutes, stirring constantly.
9. Pour in the coconut milk, chicken or vegetable broth, and diced tomatoes. Stir to combine.
10. Add the diced potatoes to the skillet and bring the mixture to a simmer. Let it cook for 10-15 minutes, or until the potatoes are tender.
11. Stir in the green peas and sous vide dove breasts. Simmer for another 5-10 minutes to heat through.
12. Season the curry with salt and pepper to taste.
13. Serve the sous vide dove curry hot, garnished with chopped fresh cilantro. Serve with cooked rice or naan bread on the side.

Nutritional information: (per serving) 450 calories, 30g protein, 25g carbohydrates, 25g fat, 6g fiber, 70mg cholesterol, 800mg sodium, 600mg potassium

Chapter 6 Seafood and fish

Fish

Sous Vide Lemon Herb Salmon

Yield: 4 servings | Prep time: 10 minutes | Cook time: 40 minutes
Ingredients:

- 4 salmon fillets, skin-on, about 6 ounces each
- Salt and black pepper, to taste
- 2 tablespoons olive oil
- 2 cloves garlic, minced
- Zest of 1 lemon
- Juice of 1 lemon
- 2 tablespoons chopped fresh dill
- 2 tablespoons chopped fresh parsley

Directions:

1. Preheat the sous vide water bath to 130°F (54°C).
2. Season the salmon fillets with salt and pepper on both sides.
3. In a small bowl, mix the olive oil, minced garlic, lemon zest, lemon juice, chopped dill, and chopped parsley to make the marinade.
4. Place each seasoned salmon fillet in a separate vacuum-sealed bag. Divide the marinade evenly among the bags, pouring it over the salmon.
5. Seal the bags using a vacuum sealer and place them in the preheated water bath. Cook the salmon for 30-40 minutes.
6. Once the salmon is cooked, remove it from the bags and pat dry with paper towels.
7. Heat a skillet over medium-high heat. Add a little olive oil and sear the salmon fillets, skin side down, for 1-2 minutes until crispy.

Nutritional information: 350 calories, 36g protein, 2g carbohydrates, 22g fat, 1g fiber, 90mg cholesterol, 120mg sodium, 600mg potassium

Sous Vide Mediterranean Salmon

Yield: 4 servings | Prep time: 15 minutes | Cook time: 40 minutes
Ingredients:

- 4 salmon fillets, skin-on, about 6 ounces each
- Salt and black pepper, to taste
- 2 tablespoons olive oil
- 2 cloves garlic, minced
- 1 teaspoon dried oregano

- 1 teaspoon dried thyme
- Zest of 1 lemon
- Juice of 1 lemon
- 1/4 cup chopped sun-dried tomatoes
- 1/4 cup sliced Kalamata olives
- 2 tablespoons chopped fresh parsley

Directions:

1. Preheat the sous vide water bath to 130°F (54°C).
2. Season the salmon fillets with salt and pepper on both sides.
3. In a small bowl, mix the olive oil, minced garlic, dried oregano, dried thyme, lemon zest, lemon juice, sun-dried tomatoes, Kalamata olives, and chopped parsley.
4. Place each seasoned salmon fillet in a separate vacuum-sealed bag. Divide the olive oil mixture evenly among the bags, pouring it over the salmon.
5. Seal the bags using a vacuum sealer and place them in the preheated water bath. Cook the salmon for 30-40 minutes.
6. Once the salmon is cooked, remove it from the bags and pat dry with paper towels.
7. Serve the salmon with additional lemon wedges and garnish with fresh parsley, if desired.

Nutritional information: 380 calories, 36g protein, 4g carbohydrates, 25g fat, 1g fiber, 90mg cholesterol, 350mg sodium, 600mg potassium

Sous Vide Smoked Salmon

Yield: 4 servings | Prep time: 10 minutes | Cook time: 2 hours
Ingredients:

- 1 lb (450g) salmon fillet, skin-on
- 1/4 cup (60ml) maple syrup
- 2 tablespoons (30ml) soy sauce
- 1 tablespoon (15ml) liquid smoke
- 1 teaspoon (5ml) garlic powder
- 1 teaspoon (5ml) onion powder
- Salt and black pepper, to taste

Directions:

1. Preheat the sous vide water bath to 125°F (52°C).
2. In a small bowl, whisk together the maple syrup, soy sauce, liquid smoke, garlic powder, and onion powder.
3. Place the salmon fillet in a large vacuum-sealed bag. Pour the maple syrup mixture over the salmon, ensuring it is evenly coated. Season with salt and pepper.
4. Seal the bag using a vacuum sealer, making sure to remove any air pockets.
5. Submerge the bag in the preheated water bath and cook for 2 hours.
6. Once cooked, remove the bag from the water bath and carefully open it. Remove the salmon from the bag and pat it dry with paper towels.
7. Optionally, you can finish the salmon by briefly searing it in a hot skillet or using a culinary torch for added flavor and texture.

Nutritional information: 250 calories, 25g protein, 10g carbohydrates, 12g fat, 0g fiber, 60mg cholesterol, 400mg sodium, 450mg potassium

Sous Vide Coconut Curry Salmon

Yield: 4 servings | Prep time: 15 minutes | Cook time: 1 hour

Ingredients:

- 4 salmon fillets, skin-on, about 6 ounces each
- Salt and black pepper, to taste
- 1 tablespoon olive oil
- 1 onion, finely chopped
- 2 cloves garlic, minced
- 1 tablespoon curry powder
- 1 teaspoon ground turmeric
- 1 can (13.5 oz) coconut milk
- 1 tablespoon fish sauce
- Juice of 1 lime
- 2 tablespoons chopped fresh cilantro

Directions:

1. Preheat the sous vide water bath to 125°F (52°C).
2. Season the salmon fillets with salt and pepper on both sides.
3. In a large skillet, heat the olive oil over medium heat. Add the chopped onion and garlic, and sauté until softened, about 5 minutes.
4. Stir in the curry powder and ground turmeric, and cook for another minute until fragrant.
5. Add the coconut milk and fish sauce to the skillet, and bring to a simmer. Cook for 5 minutes, stirring occasionally.
6. Remove the skillet from the heat and stir in the lime juice and chopped cilantro.
7. Place each seasoned salmon fillet in a separate vacuum-sealed bag. Divide the coconut curry mixture evenly among the bags, pouring it over the salmon.
8. Seal the bags using a vacuum sealer and place them in the preheated water bath. Cook the salmon for 1 hour.
9. Once cooked, remove the bags from the water bath and carefully open them. Serve the salmon with additional chopped cilantro on top.

Nutritional information: 380 calories, 36g protein, 6g carbohydrates, 25g fat, 1g fiber, 90mg cholesterol, 300mg sodium, 550mg potassium

Sous Vide Garlic Butter Salmon

Yield: 4 servings | Prep time: 10 minutes | Cook time: 1 hour

Ingredients:

- 4 salmon fillets, skin-on, about 6 ounces each
- Salt and black pepper, to taste
- 4 tablespoons unsalted butter
- 4 cloves garlic, minced
- 2 tablespoons chopped fresh parsley
- 1 tablespoon lemon juice
- Lemon slices, for serving
- Fresh parsley, for garnish

Directions:

1. Preheat the sous vide water bath to 125°F (52°C).
2. Season the salmon fillets with salt and pepper on both sides.
3. In a small saucepan, melt the butter over low heat. Add the minced garlic and cook for 2-3 minutes until fragrant.
4. Stir in the chopped parsley and lemon juice. Remove from heat and let the garlic butter mixture cool slightly.
5. Place each seasoned salmon fillet in a separate vacuum-sealed bag. Divide the garlic butter mixture evenly among the bags, pouring it over the salmon.
6. Seal the bags using a vacuum sealer and place them in the preheated water bath. Cook the salmon for 1 hour.
7. Once cooked, remove the bags from the water bath and carefully open them. Serve the salmon with lemon slices and garnish with fresh parsley.

Nutritional information: 400 calories, 36g protein, 2g carbohydrates, 27g fat, 0g fiber, 110mg cholesterol, 150mg sodium, 550mg potassium

Sous Vide Halibut with Lemon Butter Sauce

Yield: 4 servings | Prep time: 15 minutes | Cook time: 1 hour

Ingredients:

- 4 halibut fillets, about 6 ounces each
- Salt and black pepper, to taste
- 4 tablespoons unsalted butter
- 2 cloves garlic, minced
- Zest of 1 lemon
- Juice of 1 lemon
- 2 tablespoons chopped fresh parsley
- Lemon slices, for serving

Directions:

1. Preheat the sous vide water bath to 130°F (54°C).
2. Season the halibut fillets with salt and pepper on both sides.
3. Place each seasoned halibut fillet in a separate vacuum-sealed bag.
4. Seal the bags using a vacuum sealer and place them in the preheated water bath. Cook the halibut for 1 hour.
5. In a small saucepan, melt the butter over low heat. Add the minced garlic and cook for 2-3 minutes until fragrant.
6. Stir in the lemon zest, lemon juice, and chopped parsley. Remove from heat and set aside.
7. Once the halibut is cooked, remove the bags from the water bath and carefully open them. Transfer the halibut fillets to serving plates.
8. Spoon the lemon butter sauce over the halibut fillets.
9. Serve the halibut with lemon slices on the side.

Nutritional information: 350 calories, 30g protein, 1g carbohydrates, 25g fat, 0g fiber, 100mg cholesterol, 120mg sodium, 600mg potassium

Sous Vide Halibut with Capers and White Wine

Yield: 4 servings | Prep time: 15 minutes | Cook time: 1 hour

Ingredients:

- 4 halibut fillets, about 6 ounces each
- Salt and black pepper, to taste
- 4 tablespoons unsalted butter
- 2 cloves garlic, minced

- 1/4 cup white wine
- 2 tablespoons capers, drained
- Zest of 1 lemon
- Juice of 1 lemon
- 2 tablespoons chopped fresh parsley

Directions:

1. Preheat the sous vide water bath to 130°F (54°C).
2. Season the halibut fillets with salt and pepper on both sides.
3. Place each seasoned halibut fillet in a separate vacuum-sealed bag.
4. Seal the bags using a vacuum sealer and place them in the preheated water bath. Cook the halibut for 1 hour.
5. In a skillet, melt the butter over medium heat. Add the minced garlic and cook for 1 minute until fragrant.
6. Pour in the white wine and bring to a simmer. Cook for 2-3 minutes until slightly reduced.
7. Stir in the capers, lemon zest, and lemon juice. Remove from heat and set aside.
8. Once the halibut is cooked, remove the bags from the water bath and carefully open them. Transfer the halibut fillets to serving plates.
9. Spoon the caper and white wine sauce over the halibut fillets.
10. Garnish with chopped parsley and serve immediately.

Nutritional information: 350 calories, 30g protein, 2g carbohydrates, 25g fat, 0g fiber, 100mg cholesterol, 300mg sodium, 600mg potassium

Sous Vide Halibut with Mango Salsa

Yield: 4 servings | Prep time: 20 minutes | Cook time: 1 hour
Ingredients:

- 4 halibut fillets, about 6 ounces each
- Salt and black pepper, to taste
- 2 tablespoons olive oil
- 2 ripe mangoes, peeled, pitted, and diced
- 1 red bell pepper, diced
- 1/2 red onion, finely chopped
- 1 jalapeño pepper, seeded and minced
- Juice of 2 limes
- 2 tablespoons chopped fresh cilantro
- Salt, to taste

Directions:

1. Preheat the sous vide water bath to 130°F (54°C).
2. Season the halibut fillets with salt and pepper on both sides.
3. Place each seasoned halibut fillet in a separate vacuum-sealed bag.
4. Seal the bags using a vacuum sealer and place them in the preheated water bath. Cook the halibut for 1 hour.
5. While the halibut is cooking, prepare the mango salsa. In a medium bowl, combine the diced mangoes, red bell pepper, red onion, jalapeño pepper, lime juice, and chopped cilantro. Season with salt to taste and toss to combine. Refrigerate until ready to serve.
6. Once the halibut is cooked, remove the bags from the water bath and carefully open them. Transfer the halibut fillets to serving plates.
7. Spoon the mango salsa over the halibut fillets.
8. Serve immediately, garnished with additional cilantro if desired.

Nutritional information: 350 calories, 30g protein, 20g carbohydrates, 15g fat, 3g fiber, 80mg cholesterol, 150mg sodium, 700mg potassium

Sous Vide Halibut with Tomato Basil Relish

Yield: 4 servings | Prep time: 20 minutes | Cook time: 1 hour

Ingredients:

- 4 halibut fillets, about 6 ounces each
- Salt and black pepper, to taste
- 2 tablespoons olive oil
- 2 cups cherry tomatoes, halved
- 1/4 cup chopped fresh basil
- 2 cloves garlic, minced
- 2 tablespoons balsamic vinegar
- 1 tablespoon olive oil
- Salt and black pepper, to taste

Directions:

1. Preheat the sous vide water bath to 130°F (54°C).
2. Season the halibut fillets with salt and pepper on both sides.
3. Place each seasoned halibut fillet in a separate vacuum-sealed bag.
4. Seal the bags using a vacuum sealer and place them in the preheated water bath. Cook the halibut for 1 hour.
5. While the halibut is cooking, prepare the tomato basil relish. In a medium bowl, combine the halved cherry tomatoes, chopped basil, minced garlic, balsamic vinegar, and olive oil. Season with salt and pepper to taste. Toss to combine and set aside.
6. Once the halibut is cooked, remove the bags from the water bath and carefully open them. Transfer the halibut fillets to serving plates.
7. Spoon the tomato basil relish over the halibut fillets.
8. Serve immediately, garnished with additional fresh basil if desired.

Nutritional information: 300 calories, 30g protein, 8g carbohydrates, 15g fat, 2g fiber, 70mg cholesterol, 200mg sodium, 600mg potassium

Sous Vide Tuna Nicoise Salad

Yield: 4 servings | Prep time: 20 minutes | Cook time: 1 hour

Ingredients:

- 4 tuna steaks, about 6 ounces each
- Salt and black pepper, to taste
- 2 tablespoons olive oil
- 4 large eggs
- 1 pound small potatoes, halved
- 1/2 pound green beans, trimmed
- 1 cup cherry tomatoes, halved
- 1/4 cup Kalamata olives, pitted
- 2 tablespoons capers
- 4 cups mixed salad greens

- 1/4 cup chopped fresh parsley
- Lemon wedges, for serving

For the vinaigrette:

- 1/4 cup olive oil
- 2 tablespoons red wine vinegar
- 1 teaspoon Dijon mustard
- 1 teaspoon minced garlic
- Salt and black pepper, to taste

Directions:

1. Preheat the sous vide water bath to 125°F (52°C).
2. Season the tuna steaks with salt and pepper on both sides.
3. Place each seasoned tuna steak in a separate vacuum-sealed bag. Drizzle each with a little olive oil. Seal the bags using a vacuum sealer.
4. In a separate pot of boiling water, cook the eggs for 7 minutes. Transfer the eggs to a bowl of ice water to cool, then peel and halve them.
5. In another vacuum-sealed bag, place the halved potatoes and green beans. Season with salt and pepper and drizzle with olive oil. Seal the bag.
6. Place the bags of tuna, potatoes, and green beans in the preheated water bath. Cook the tuna for 45 minutes and the potatoes and green beans for 1 hour.
7. While the ingredients are cooking, prepare the vinaigrette by whisking together the olive oil, red wine vinegar, Dijon mustard, minced garlic, salt, and pepper in a small bowl.
8. Once cooked, remove the bags from the water bath and carefully open them. Arrange the mixed salad greens on serving plates and top with the cooked potatoes, green beans, cherry tomatoes, Kalamata olives, capers, and chopped parsley.
9. Slice the sous vide tuna and place it on top of the salad. Arrange the halved boiled eggs around the plate.
10. Drizzle the vinaigrette over the salad and serve with lemon wedges on the side.

Nutritional information: 450 calories, 40g protein, 20g carbohydrates, 25g fat, 5g fiber, 300mg cholesterol, 500mg sodium, 800mg potassium

Sous Vide Tuna Carpaccio

Yield: 4 servings | Prep time: 15 minutes | Cook time: 1 hour

Ingredients:

- 1 lb sushi-grade tuna loin
- 2 tablespoons olive oil
- 1 tablespoon soy sauce
- 1 tablespoon lemon juice
- 1 teaspoon minced garlic
- 1 teaspoon grated ginger
- Salt and black pepper, to taste
- 1 tablespoon sesame seeds, for garnish
- 2 green onions, thinly sliced, for garnish
- 1 tablespoon chopped fresh cilantro, for garnish

Directions:

1. Preheat the sous vide water bath to 115°F (46°C).
2. Slice the tuna loin into thin slices, about 1/8 inch thick.

3. In a small bowl, whisk together the olive oil, soy sauce, lemon juice, minced garlic, grated ginger, salt, and black pepper to make the marinade.
4. Place the tuna slices in a single layer in a shallow dish or a vacuum-sealed bag. Pour the marinade over the tuna slices, making sure they are evenly coated. If using a shallow dish, cover with plastic wrap. If using a vacuum-sealed bag, remove the air and seal.
5. Place the dish or bag in the preheated water bath and cook for 1 hour.
6. Once the tuna is cooked, remove it from the water bath and carefully arrange the slices on serving plates.
7. Drizzle any remaining marinade over the tuna slices.
8. Garnish with sesame seeds, sliced green onions, and chopped cilantro.
9. Serve immediately as an appetizer or starter.

Nutritional information: 200 calories, 25g protein, 2g carbohydrates, 10g fat, 0g fiber, 50mg cholesterol, 300mg sodium, 400mg potassium

Sous Vide Tuna with Chimichurri Sauce

Yield: 4 servings | Prep time: 15 minutes | Cook time: 1 hour

Ingredients:

- 4 tuna steaks, about 6 ounces each
- Salt and black pepper, to taste
- 2 tablespoons olive oil
- 1/4 cup fresh parsley, chopped
- 1/4 cup fresh cilantro, chopped
- 2 cloves garlic, minced
- 1 shallot, minced
- 1/4 cup red wine vinegar
- 1/2 cup olive oil
- 1 teaspoon dried oregano
- 1/2 teaspoon red pepper flakes
- Salt and black pepper, to taste

Directions:

1. Preheat the sous vide water bath to 125°F (52°C).
2. Season the tuna steaks with salt and pepper on both sides.
3. Place each seasoned tuna steak in a separate vacuum-sealed bag. Drizzle each with a little olive oil. Seal the bags using a vacuum sealer.
4. In a blender or food processor, combine the chopped parsley, chopped cilantro, minced garlic, minced shallot, red wine vinegar, olive oil, dried oregano, red pepper flakes, salt, and black pepper. Blend until smooth to make the chimichurri sauce.
5. Place the bags of tuna in the preheated water bath. Cook the tuna for 1 hour.
6. Once cooked, remove the bags from the water bath and carefully open them. Transfer the tuna steaks to serving plates.
7. Spoon the chimichurri sauce over the tuna steaks.
8. Serve immediately, garnished with additional chopped parsley or cilantro if desired.

Nutritional information: 350 calories, 40g protein, 2g carbohydrates, 20g fat, 1g fiber, 70mg cholesterol, 300mg sodium, 500mg potassium

Sous Vide Trout with Spinach and Feta

Yield: 4 servings | Prep time: 15 minutes | Cook time: 1 hour

Ingredients:

- 4 trout fillets, about 6 ounces each
- Salt and black pepper, to taste
- 2 tablespoons olive oil
- 4 cups fresh baby spinach
- 1/2 cup crumbled feta cheese
- 2 cloves garlic, minced
- 1/4 teaspoon red pepper flakes
- Juice of 1 lemon

Directions:

1. Preheat the sous vide water bath to 125°F (52°C).
2. Season the trout fillets with salt and black pepper on both sides.
3. Place each seasoned trout fillet in a separate vacuum-sealed bag. Drizzle each with a little olive oil. Seal the bags using a vacuum sealer.
4. Place the bags of trout in the preheated water bath. Cook the trout for 1 hour.
5. While the trout is cooking, heat 1 tablespoon of olive oil in a skillet over medium heat. Add the minced garlic and red pepper flakes, and cook for 1 minute until fragrant.
6. Add the fresh baby spinach to the skillet and cook, stirring occasionally, until wilted, about 2-3 minutes.
7. Once the trout is cooked, remove the bags from the water bath and carefully open them. Transfer the trout fillets to serving plates.
8. Divide the sautéed spinach evenly among the plates, placing it alongside the trout fillets.
9. Sprinkle the crumbled feta cheese over the trout and spinach.
10. Drizzle the lemon juice over the trout and spinach.
11. Serve immediately.

Nutritional information: 300 calories, 25g protein, 4g carbohydrates, 20g fat, 1g fiber, 80mg cholesterol, 400mg sodium, 600mg potassium

Sous Vide Trout with Pesto Crust

Yield: 4 servings | Prep time: 15 minutes | Cook time: 1 hour

Ingredients:

- 4 trout fillets, about 6 ounces each
- Salt and black pepper, to taste
- 1/4 cup basil pesto
- 1/4 cup breadcrumbs
- 2 tablespoons grated Parmesan cheese
- 1 tablespoon olive oil

Directions:

1. Preheat the sous vide water bath to 125°F (52°C).
2. Season the trout fillets with salt and black pepper on both sides.
3. In a small bowl, combine the basil pesto, breadcrumbs, and grated Parmesan cheese to make the pesto crust mixture.

4. Place each seasoned trout fillet in a separate vacuum-sealed bag. Spread a layer of the pesto crust mixture evenly over each fillet. Seal the bags using a vacuum sealer.
5. Place the bags of trout in the preheated water bath. Cook the trout for 1 hour.
6. After the trout has cooked, remove the bags from the water bath and carefully open them.
7. Heat the olive oil in a skillet over medium-high heat. Carefully transfer each trout fillet to the skillet, crust-side down, and sear for 1-2 minutes until the crust is golden brown and crispy.
8. Serve the trout fillets immediately, with additional pesto if desired.

Nutritional information: 350 calories, 25g protein, 5g carbohydrates, 25g fat, 1g fiber, 80mg cholesterol, 450mg sodium, 550mg potassium

Sous Vide Trout with Sesame Soy Glaze

Yield: 4 servings | Prep time: 15 minutes | Cook time: 1 hour

Ingredients:

- 4 trout fillets, about 6 ounces each
- Salt and black pepper, to taste
- 2 tablespoons sesame oil
- 2 tablespoons soy sauce
- 2 tablespoons honey
- 1 tablespoon rice vinegar
- 1 tablespoon minced ginger
- 1 clove garlic, minced
- 1 tablespoon sesame seeds, for garnish
- 2 green onions, thinly sliced, for garnish

Directions:

1. Preheat the sous vide water bath to 125°F (52°C).
2. Season the trout fillets with salt and black pepper on both sides.
3. In a small bowl, whisk together the sesame oil, soy sauce, honey, rice vinegar, minced ginger, and minced garlic to make the sesame soy glaze.
4. Place each seasoned trout fillet in a separate vacuum-sealed bag. Pour the sesame soy glaze over each fillet. Seal the bags using a vacuum sealer.
5. Place the bags of trout in the preheated water bath. Cook the trout for 1 hour.
6. After the trout has cooked, remove the bags from the water bath and carefully open them.
7. Heat a skillet over medium-high heat. Carefully transfer each trout fillet to the skillet, skin-side down, and sear for 1-2 minutes until the skin is crispy.
8. Serve the trout fillets immediately, garnished with sesame seeds and sliced green onions.

Nutritional information: 350 calories, 25g protein, 15g carbohydrates, 20g fat, 1g fiber, 80mg cholesterol, 600mg sodium, 500mg potassium

Sous Vide Cod with Mediterranean Vegetables

Yield: 4 servings | Prep time: 15 minutes | Cook time: 1 hour

Ingredients:

- 4 cod fillets, about 6 ounces each
- Salt and black pepper, to taste
- 2 tablespoons olive oil

- 1 red bell pepper, sliced
- 1 yellow bell pepper, sliced
- 1 small eggplant, diced
- 1 zucchini, sliced
- 1 yellow squash, sliced
- 1 onion, sliced
- 2 cloves garlic, minced
- 1 teaspoon dried oregano
- 1 teaspoon dried basil
- Salt and black pepper, to taste
- 1/4 cup chopped fresh parsley, for garnish

Directions:

1. Preheat the sous vide water bath to 130°F (54°C).
2. Season the cod fillets with salt and black pepper on both sides.
3. Place each seasoned cod fillet in a separate vacuum-sealed bag. Drizzle each with a little olive oil. Seal the bags using a vacuum sealer.
4. In a large bowl, toss together the sliced red bell pepper, yellow bell pepper, diced eggplant, sliced zucchini, sliced yellow squash, sliced onion, minced garlic, dried oregano, dried basil, salt, and black pepper.
5. Divide the mixed vegetables evenly among four vacuum-sealed bags. Seal the bags using a vacuum sealer.
6. Place the bags of cod and vegetables in the preheated water bath. Cook the cod for 1 hour and the vegetables for 1 hour.
7. After the cod and vegetables have cooked, remove the bags from the water bath and carefully open them.
8. Divide the cooked vegetables among serving plates. Top each plate with a cooked cod fillet.
9. Garnish with chopped fresh parsley.
10. Serve immediately.

Nutritional information: 250 calories, 25g protein, 15g carbohydrates, 10g fat, 5g fiber, 50mg cholesterol, 300mg sodium, 800mg potassium

Sous Vide Cod with Spinach and Tomatoes

Yield: 4 servings | Prep time: 15 minutes | Cook time: 1 hour

Ingredients:

- 4 cod fillets, about 6 ounces each
- Salt and black pepper, to taste
- 2 tablespoons olive oil
- 2 cups cherry tomatoes, halved
- 4 cups fresh baby spinach
- 2 cloves garlic, minced
- 1 tablespoon balsamic vinegar
- 1 teaspoon dried thyme
- Salt and black pepper, to taste
- Lemon wedges, for serving

Directions:

1. Preheat the sous vide water bath to 130°F (54°C).
2. Season the cod fillets with salt and black pepper on both sides.

3. Place each seasoned cod fillet in a separate vacuum-sealed bag. Drizzle each with a little olive oil. Seal the bags using a vacuum sealer.
4. In a large bowl, toss together the halved cherry tomatoes, fresh baby spinach, minced garlic, balsamic vinegar, dried thyme, salt, and black pepper.
5. Divide the tomato and spinach mixture evenly among four vacuum-sealed bags. Seal the bags using a vacuum sealer.
6. Place the bags of cod and vegetables in the preheated water bath. Cook the cod for 1 hour and the vegetables for 1 hour.
7. After the cod and vegetables have cooked, remove the bags from the water bath and carefully open them.
8. Divide the cooked vegetables among serving plates. Top each plate with a cooked cod fillet.
9. Serve immediately with lemon wedges on the side.

Nutritional information: 300 calories, 25g protein, 10g carbohydrates, 15g fat, 3g fiber, 50mg cholesterol, 300mg sodium, 700mg potassium

Simple Sous Vide Sea Bass

Yield: 4 servings | Prep time: 10 minutes | Cook time: 40 minutes
Ingredients:

- 4 sea bass fillets (about 6 ounces each)
- 2 tablespoons olive oil
- 4 cloves garlic, minced
- 2 tablespoons fresh lemon juice
- 1 teaspoon lemon zest
- Salt and pepper to taste
- Fresh herbs (such as thyme or rosemary), for garnish

Directions:

1. Preheat the sous vide water bath to 140°F (60°C).
2. Season the sea bass fillets generously with salt and pepper.
3. Place the seasoned sea bass fillets in a single layer in a vacuum-sealable bag or a zip-top bag.
4. Add olive oil, minced garlic, lemon juice, and lemon zest to the bag with the sea bass.
5. Seal the bag using a vacuum sealer or the water displacement method.
6. Gently lower the bag into the preheated water bath, ensuring the fish is fully submerged.
7. Cook the sea bass for 30-40 minutes.
8. Once cooked, carefully remove the sea bass from the bag and pat dry with paper towels.
9. Optionally, you can sear the sea bass in a hot skillet for a minute on each side for added color and flavor.
10. Serve the sous vide sea bass garnished with fresh herbs and additional lemon wedges if desired.

Nutritional information: Approximately 250 calories, 30g protein, 2g carbohydrates, 14g fat, 0g fiber, 80mg cholesterol, 300mg sodium, 500mg potassium

Asian-Inspired Sous Vide Sea Bass

Yield: 4 servings | Prep time: 15 minutes | Cook time: 40 minutes
Ingredients:

- 4 sea bass fillets (about 6 ounces each)
- 1/4 cup soy sauce
- 2 tablespoons rice vinegar

- 2 tablespoons honey
- 1 tablespoon sesame oil
- 2 cloves garlic, minced
- 1 teaspoon fresh ginger, grated
- 2 green onions, thinly sliced
- Sesame seeds, for garnish
- Cooked rice or steamed vegetables, for serving

Directions:

1. Preheat the sous vide water bath to 140°F (60°C).
2. In a bowl, whisk together soy sauce, rice vinegar, honey, sesame oil, minced garlic, grated ginger, and sliced green onions to make the marinade.
3. Season the sea bass fillets with salt and pepper.
4. Place the sea bass fillets in a single layer in a vacuum-sealable bag or a zip-top bag.
5. Pour the marinade over the sea bass fillets, ensuring they are evenly coated.
6. Seal the bag using a vacuum sealer or the water displacement method.
7. Gently lower the bag into the preheated water bath, ensuring the fish is fully submerged.
8. Cook the sea bass for 30-40 minutes.
9. Once cooked, carefully remove the sea bass from the bag and pat dry with paper towels.
10. Optionally, you can sear the sea bass in a hot skillet for a minute on each side for added color and flavor.
11. Serve the sous vide sea bass over cooked rice or alongside steamed vegetables, garnished with sesame seeds.

Nutritional information: Approximately 280 calories, 30g protein, 10g carbohydrates, 12g fat, 1g fiber, 70mg cholesterol, 1000mg sodium, 350mg potassium

Miso-Glazed Sous Vide Sea Bass

Yield: 4 servings | Prep time: 15 minutes | Cook time: 40 minutes
Ingredients:

- 4 sea bass fillets (about 6 ounces each)
- 1/4 cup white miso paste
- 2 tablespoons mirin
- 2 tablespoons sake
- 2 tablespoons brown sugar
- 2 tablespoons soy sauce
- 2 cloves garlic, minced
- 1 teaspoon grated ginger
- Sesame seeds and sliced green onions, for garnish
- Cooked rice or steamed vegetables, for serving

Directions:

1. Preheat the sous vide water bath to 140°F (60°C).
2. In a bowl, whisk together white miso paste, mirin, sake, brown sugar, soy sauce, minced garlic, and grated ginger to make the glaze.
3. Season the sea bass fillets with salt and pepper.
4. Place the sea bass fillets in a single layer in a vacuum-sealable bag or a zip-top bag.
5. Pour the miso glaze over the sea bass fillets, ensuring they are evenly coated.
6. Seal the bag using a vacuum sealer or the water displacement method.
7. Gently lower the bag into the preheated water bath, ensuring the fish is fully submerged.

8. Cook the sea bass for 30-40 minutes.
9. Once cooked, carefully remove the sea bass from the bag and pat dry with paper towels.
10. Optionally, you can sear the sea bass in a hot skillet for a minute on each side for added color and flavor.
11. Serve the sous vide sea bass over cooked rice or alongside steamed vegetables, garnished with sesame seeds and sliced green onions.

Nutritional information: Approximately 290 calories, 30g protein, 12g carbohydrates, 10g fat, 1g fiber, 70mg cholesterol, 800mg sodium, 400mg potassium

Sous Vide Catfish Etouffee

Yield: 4 servings | Prep time: 15 minutes | Cook time: 2 hours
Ingredients:

- 4 catfish fillets
- 2 tablespoons olive oil
- 1 onion, diced
- 1 bell pepper, diced
- 2 celery stalks, diced
- 3 cloves garlic, minced
- 1 can (14.5 oz) diced tomatoes
- 1 cup seafood or chicken broth
- 2 tablespoons tomato paste
- 1 tablespoon Cajun seasoning
- 1 teaspoon dried thyme
- 1 teaspoon paprika
- 1/2 teaspoon cayenne pepper (optional)
- Salt and pepper to taste
- 2 tablespoons butter
- 2 tablespoons all-purpose flour
- 2 green onions, chopped (for garnish)
- Cooked rice, for serving

Directions:

1. Preheat the sous vide water bath to 135°F (57°C).
2. Season catfish fillets with salt, pepper, and Cajun seasoning. Place them in a vacuum-sealed bag and seal.
3. Cook catfish in the sous vide water bath for 1 hour.
4. While the catfish is cooking, heat olive oil in a skillet over medium heat. Add onion, bell pepper, and celery. Sauté until vegetables are softened, about 5-7 minutes.
5. Add minced garlic and cook for another minute.
6. Stir in diced tomatoes, broth, tomato paste, Cajun seasoning, thyme, paprika, and cayenne pepper. Bring to a simmer and let it cook for 10-15 minutes, allowing flavors to meld.
7. In a separate small saucepan, melt butter over medium heat. Stir in flour to create a roux. Cook, stirring constantly, until the roux is golden brown, about 3-5 minutes.
8. Gradually whisk the roux into the tomato mixture until well combined and thickened. Simmer for an additional 5 minutes.
9. Once the catfish is done cooking, remove it from the sous vide bag and flake it into bite-sized pieces. Add the catfish to the etouffee sauce, stirring gently to combine.
10. Serve the catfish etouffee over cooked rice, garnished with chopped green onions.

Nutritional information: (per serving) 315 calories, 27g protein, 18g carbohydrates, 15g fat, 3g fiber, 82mg cholesterol, 670mg sodium, 580mg potassium

Simple Sous Vide Catfish

Yield: 4 servings | Prep time: 10 minutes | Cook time: 1 hour
Ingredients:

- 4 catfish fillets
- Salt and pepper to taste
- 2 tablespoons olive oil

Directions:

1. Preheat the sous vide water bath to 135°F (57°C).
2. Season catfish fillets generously with salt and pepper on both sides.
3. Place the seasoned catfish fillets in a single layer in a vacuum-sealed bag. Drizzle with olive oil.
4. Seal the bag using a vacuum sealer or the water displacement method.
5. Submerge the sealed bag in the preheated water bath and cook for 1 hour.
6. Once the cooking time is up, remove the bag from the water bath and carefully take out the catfish fillets.
7. Pat the catfish fillets dry with paper towels.
8. Heat a skillet over medium-high heat and add a tablespoon of olive oil.
9. Sear the catfish fillets for 1-2 minutes on each side, or until lightly browned.
10. Serve immediately, garnished with fresh herbs or a squeeze of lemon if desired.

Nutritional information: (per serving) 220 calories, 25g protein, 0g carbohydrates, 13g fat, 0g fiber, 80mg cholesterol, 320mg sodium, 380mg potassium

Seafood

Basic Sous Vide Octopus

Yield: 4 servings | Prep time: 15 minutes | Cook time: 4 hours
Ingredients:

- 2 pounds octopus, cleaned and tentacles separated
- 2 tablespoons olive oil
- 4 cloves garlic, minced
- 1 lemon, sliced
- Salt and pepper to taste

Directions:

1. Preheat the sous vide water bath to 185°F (85°C).
2. Rinse the octopus under cold water and pat dry with paper towels.
3. Season the octopus with salt, pepper, and minced garlic, rubbing it all over the tentacles.
4. Place the seasoned octopus and lemon slices in a vacuum-sealed bag. Drizzle with olive oil.
5. Seal the bag using a vacuum sealer or the water displacement method.
6. Submerge the sealed bag in the preheated water bath and cook for 4 hours.
7. Once the cooking time is up, carefully remove the bag from the water bath and take out the octopus.

8. Heat a grill or grill pan over high heat.
9. Remove the octopus from the bag and pat dry with paper towels.
10. Grill the octopus for 2-3 minutes on each side, until lightly charred and heated through.
11. Serve the grilled octopus immediately, drizzled with additional olive oil and lemon juice if desired.

Nutritional information: (per serving) 180 calories, 25g protein, 2g carbohydrates, 8g fat, 0g fiber, 85mg cholesterol, 500mg sodium, 600mg potassium

Sous Vide Octopus Paella

Yield: 4 servings | Prep time: 20 minutes | Cook time: 4 hours
Ingredients:

- 2 pounds octopus, cleaned and tentacles separated
- 1 cup Arborio rice
- 4 cups chicken or seafood broth
- 1 onion, finely chopped
- 3 cloves garlic, minced
- 1 red bell pepper, diced
- 1 yellow bell pepper, diced
- 1 cup frozen peas
- 1 teaspoon smoked paprika
- 1 teaspoon saffron threads
- Salt and pepper to taste
- 2 tablespoons olive oil
- Lemon wedges, for serving
- Chopped parsley, for garnish

Directions:

1. Preheat the sous vide water bath to 185°F (85°C).
2. Season the octopus with salt and pepper.
3. Place the octopus in a vacuum-sealed bag and add 1 tablespoon of olive oil. Seal the bag.
4. Submerge the sealed bag in the preheated water bath and cook for 4 hours.
5. After 3 hours of octopus cooking time, prepare the paella. In a large skillet, heat 1 tablespoon of olive oil over medium heat.
6. Add the chopped onion and garlic, and sauté until softened, about 3-4 minutes.
7. Stir in the diced bell peppers and cook for another 2-3 minutes.
8. Add the Arborio rice to the skillet and toast it for 2 minutes, stirring constantly.
9. Sprinkle in the smoked paprika and saffron threads, and stir to combine.
10. Pour in the chicken or seafood broth and bring to a simmer. Cook for 15-20 minutes, stirring occasionally, until the rice is almost tender and the liquid is mostly absorbed.
11. Stir in the frozen peas and cook for an additional 5 minutes.
12. Once the octopus is done cooking, remove it from the sous vide bag and pat dry with paper towels. Cut the octopus into bite-sized pieces.
13. Fold the octopus pieces into the paella mixture.
14. Season with additional salt and pepper if needed.
15. Serve the octopus paella hot, garnished with chopped parsley and lemon wedges on the side.

Nutritional information: (per serving) 420 calories, 25g protein, 45g carbohydrates, 15g fat, 5g fiber, 55mg cholesterol, 900mg sodium, 800mg potassium

Sous Vide Octopus with Romesco Sauce

Yield: 4 servings | Prep time: 15 minutes | Cook time: 4 hours
Ingredients:

- 2 pounds octopus, cleaned and tentacles separated
- 2 tablespoons olive oil
- Salt and pepper to taste
- 1 cup cherry tomatoes
- 1 red bell pepper, halved and seeds removed
- 1/2 cup almonds, toasted
- 2 cloves garlic
- 2 tablespoons red wine vinegar
- 2 tablespoons extra-virgin olive oil
- 1 teaspoon smoked paprika
- Salt and pepper to taste
- Chopped parsley, for garnish
- Lemon wedges, for serving

Directions:

1. Preheat the sous vide water bath to 185°F (85°C).
2. Season the octopus with salt and pepper.
3. Place the octopus in a vacuum-sealed bag with 1 tablespoon of olive oil. Seal the bag.
4. Submerge the sealed bag in the preheated water bath and cook for 4 hours.
5. While the octopus is cooking, preheat the oven to 400°F (200°C).
6. Place the cherry tomatoes and red bell pepper halves on a baking sheet. Drizzle with olive oil and season with salt and pepper.
7. Roast in the oven for 20-25 minutes, or until the tomatoes are blistered and the pepper is softened and charred.
8. In a food processor, combine the roasted tomatoes, red bell pepper, toasted almonds, garlic, red wine vinegar, extra-virgin olive oil, and smoked paprika. Blend until smooth. Season with salt and pepper to taste.
9. Once the octopus is done cooking, remove it from the sous vide bag and pat dry with paper towels.
10. Heat a grill or grill pan over high heat. Brush the octopus with remaining olive oil and grill for 2-3 minutes on each side, until lightly charred.
11. Serve the grilled octopus with romesco sauce, garnished with chopped parsley and lemon wedges on the side.

Nutritional information: (per serving) 320 calories, 25g protein, 10g carbohydrates, 20g fat, 3g fiber, 60mg cholesterol, 450mg sodium, 700mg potassium

Sous Vide Cajun Shrimp

Yield: 4 servings | Prep time: 10 minutes | Cook time: 30 minutes
Ingredients:

- 1 pound large shrimp, peeled and deveined
- 2 tablespoons olive oil
- 2 tablespoons Cajun seasoning
- 1 teaspoon garlic powder
- 1 teaspoon smoked paprika
- 1/2 teaspoon dried thyme

- 1/2 teaspoon dried oregano
- Salt and pepper to taste
- Lemon wedges, for serving
- Chopped parsley, for garnish

Directions:

1. Preheat the sous vide water bath to 135°F (57°C).
2. In a bowl, combine the Cajun seasoning, garlic powder, smoked paprika, dried thyme, dried oregano, salt, and pepper.
3. Place the shrimp in a resealable bag and add the olive oil. Sprinkle the Cajun seasoning mixture over the shrimp. Seal the bag.
4. Submerge the sealed bag in the preheated water bath and cook for 30 minutes.
5. Once the shrimp are cooked, remove them from the sous vide bag and pat dry with paper towels.
6. Heat a skillet over medium-high heat. Add a drizzle of olive oil.
7. Sear the shrimp for 1-2 minutes on each side until lightly browned and crisp.
8. Serve the Cajun shrimp hot, garnished with chopped parsley and lemon wedges on the side.

Nutritional information: (per serving) 200 calories, 25g protein, 2g carbohydrates, 10g fat, 0g fiber, 200mg cholesterol, 600mg sodium, 300mg potassium

Sous Vide Shrimp Scampi

Yield: 4 servings | Prep time: 15 minutes | Cook time: 30 minutes

Ingredients:

- 1 pound large shrimp, peeled and deveined
- 4 tablespoons unsalted butter
- 4 cloves garlic, minced
- 1/4 cup white wine
- 1 tablespoon lemon juice
- 1 teaspoon lemon zest
- 1/4 teaspoon red pepper flakes (optional)
- Salt and pepper to taste
- 2 tablespoons chopped fresh parsley
- Cooked pasta, for serving

Directions:

1. Preheat the sous vide water bath to 135°F (57°C).
2. Season the shrimp with salt and pepper.
3. Place the seasoned shrimp in a resealable bag with 2 tablespoons of butter. Seal the bag.
4. Submerge the sealed bag in the preheated water bath and cook for 30 minutes.
5. About 10 minutes before the shrimp are done cooking, prepare the scampi sauce. In a skillet over medium heat, melt the remaining 2 tablespoons of butter.
6. Add the minced garlic and cook until fragrant, about 1-2 minutes.
7. Pour in the white wine, lemon juice, lemon zest, and red pepper flakes (if using). Let the sauce simmer for 3-4 minutes to reduce slightly.
8. Once the shrimp are cooked, remove them from the sous vide bag and pat dry with paper towels.
9. Add the cooked shrimp to the skillet with the scampi sauce. Toss to coat the shrimp in the sauce.
10. Serve the sous vide shrimp scampi over cooked pasta, garnished with chopped parsley.

Nutritional information: (per serving, excluding pasta) 280 calories, 25g protein, 3g carbohydrates, 18g fat, 0g fiber, 230mg cholesterol, 350mg sodium, 300mg potassium

Sous Vide BBQ Shrimp

Yield: 4 servings | Prep time: 10 minutes | Cook time: 30 minutes
Ingredients:

- 1 pound large shrimp, peeled and deveined
- 1/2 cup barbecue sauce
- 2 tablespoons olive oil
- 2 cloves garlic, minced
- 1 teaspoon smoked paprika
- 1/2 teaspoon onion powder
- Salt and pepper to taste
- Lemon wedges, for serving
- Chopped parsley, for garnish

Directions:

1. Preheat the sous vide water bath to 135°F (57°C).
2. In a bowl, mix the barbecue sauce, olive oil, minced garlic, smoked paprika, onion powder, salt, and pepper.
3. Place the shrimp in a resealable bag and pour the barbecue sauce mixture over them. Seal the bag.
4. Submerge the sealed bag in the preheated water bath and cook for 30 minutes.
5. Once the shrimp are cooked, remove them from the sous vide bag and pat dry with paper towels.
6. Heat a grill or grill pan over medium-high heat.
7. Grill the shrimp for 1-2 minutes on each side, or until they are lightly charred and heated through.
8. Serve the sous vide BBQ shrimp hot, garnished with chopped parsley and lemon wedges on the side.

Nutritional information: (per serving) 280 calories, 25g protein, 15g carbohydrates, 12g fat, 1g fiber, 200mg cholesterol, 550mg sodium, 320mg potassium

Sous Vide Coconut Lime Shrimp

Yield: 4 servings | Prep time: 10 minutes | Cook time: 30 minutes
Ingredients:

- 1 pound large shrimp, peeled and deveined
- 1/2 cup coconut milk
- Zest and juice of 2 limes
- 2 tablespoons soy sauce
- 2 tablespoons honey or maple syrup
- 2 cloves garlic, minced
- 1 teaspoon grated ginger
- Salt and pepper to taste
- Chopped cilantro, for garnish
- Lime wedges, for serving

Directions:

1. Preheat the sous vide water bath to 135°F (57°C).
2. In a bowl, whisk together the coconut milk, lime zest, lime juice, soy sauce, honey or maple syrup, minced garlic, grated ginger, salt, and pepper.

3. Place the shrimp in a resealable bag and pour the coconut lime marinade over them. Seal the bag.
4. Submerge the sealed bag in the preheated water bath and cook for 30 minutes.
5. Once the shrimp are cooked, remove them from the sous vide bag and pat dry with paper towels.
6. Heat a skillet over medium-high heat.
7. Sear the shrimp for 1-2 minutes on each side until lightly browned and caramelized.
8. Serve the sous vide coconut lime shrimp hot, garnished with chopped cilantro and lime wedges on the side.

Nutritional information: (per serving) 250 calories, 25g protein, 10g carbohydrates, 10g fat, 0g fiber, 200mg cholesterol, 600mg sodium, 320mg potassium

Sous Vide Garlic and Herb Grilled Shrimp

Yield: 4 servings | Prep time: 15 minutes | Cook time: 30 minutes
Ingredients:

- 1 pound large shrimp, peeled and deveined
- 3 tablespoons olive oil
- 4 cloves garlic, minced
- 2 tablespoons chopped fresh parsley
- 1 tablespoon chopped fresh basil
- 1 tablespoon chopped fresh thyme
- 1 tablespoon lemon juice
- Salt and pepper to taste
- Lemon wedges, for serving
- Chopped parsley, for garnish

Directions:

1. Preheat the sous vide water bath to 135°F (57°C).
2. In a bowl, combine the olive oil, minced garlic, chopped parsley, chopped basil, chopped thyme, lemon juice, salt, and pepper.
3. Place the shrimp in a resealable bag and pour the garlic and herb marinade over them. Seal the bag.
4. Submerge the sealed bag in the preheated water bath and cook for 30 minutes.
5. Once the shrimp are cooked, remove them from the sous vide bag and pat dry with paper towels.
6. Preheat a grill or grill pan over medium-high heat.
7. Grill the shrimp for 1-2 minutes on each side until lightly charred and heated through.
8. Serve the sous vide garlic and herb grilled shrimp hot, garnished with chopped parsley and lemon wedges on the side.

Nutritional information: (per serving) 230 calories, 25g protein, 2g carbohydrates, 14g fat, 0g fiber, 200mg cholesterol, 400mg sodium, 320mg potassium

Sous Vide Lobster Thermidor

Yield: 4 servings | Prep time: 20 minutes | Cook time: 1 hour
Ingredients:

- 2 whole lobsters (about 1 1/2 pounds each)
- 2 tablespoons butter
- 2 shallots, finely chopped
- 2 cloves garlic, minced

- 1/4 cup white wine
- 1 cup heavy cream
- 1 tablespoon Dijon mustard
- 1/4 cup grated Parmesan cheese
- 2 tablespoons chopped fresh parsley
- Salt and pepper to taste
- Lemon wedges, for serving

Directions:

1. Preheat the sous vide water bath to 140°F (60°C).
2. Split the lobsters in half lengthwise. Remove the meat from the shells, keeping the shells intact. Chop the lobster meat into bite-sized pieces.
3. Place the lobster shells in a vacuum-sealed bag and add 1 tablespoon of butter. Seal the bag.
4. Submerge the sealed bag in the preheated water bath and cook for 1 hour.
5. While the lobster shells are cooking, melt the remaining tablespoon of butter in a skillet over medium heat.
6. Add the chopped shallots and minced garlic to the skillet. Cook until softened, about 3-4 minutes.
7. Pour in the white wine and cook until reduced by half, about 2-3 minutes.
8. Stir in the heavy cream and Dijon mustard. Simmer for 5-7 minutes, until the sauce has thickened slightly.
9. Once the lobster shells are done cooking, remove them from the sous vide bag and discard them.
10. Add the chopped lobster meat to the skillet with the cream sauce. Cook for 2-3 minutes, until the lobster is heated through.
11. Stir in the grated Parmesan cheese and chopped parsley. Season with salt and pepper to taste.
12. Serve the lobster thermidor hot, garnished with additional chopped parsley and lemon wedges on the side.

Nutritional information: (per serving) 380 calories, 20g protein, 5g carbohydrates, 30g fat, 0g fiber, 220mg cholesterol, 450mg sodium, 500mg potassium

Sous Vide Lobster Ravioli

Yield: 4 servings | Prep time: 30 minutes | Cook time: 1 hour
Ingredients:

- 1 pound lobster meat, cooked and chopped
- 1/2 cup ricotta cheese
- 1/4 cup grated Parmesan cheese
- 2 cloves garlic, minced
- 1 tablespoon chopped fresh parsley
- Salt and pepper to taste
- 1 package of fresh pasta sheets
- 1 egg, beaten (for egg wash)
- Flour, for dusting
- Marinara sauce, for serving
- Chopped fresh basil, for garnish

Directions:

1. Preheat the sous vide water bath to 135°F (57°C).
2. In a bowl, combine the chopped lobster meat, ricotta cheese, grated Parmesan cheese, minced garlic, chopped parsley, salt, and pepper. Mix well to combine.
3. Lay out the fresh pasta sheets on a clean surface. Place teaspoon-sized dollops of the lobster filling evenly spaced on one sheet of pasta, leaving space between each dollop.

4. Brush the edges of the pasta sheet with beaten egg.
5. Carefully place another pasta sheet over the filling, pressing down gently to seal the edges and remove any air pockets.
6. Use a pasta cutter or knife to cut out individual ravioli squares.
7. Dust each ravioli with flour to prevent sticking.
8. Place the ravioli in a single layer in a vacuum-sealed bag. Seal the bag.
9. Submerge the sealed bag in the preheated water bath and cook for 1 hour.
10. Once the ravioli are cooked, carefully remove them from the sous vide bag and drain any excess liquid.
11. Serve the lobster ravioli hot, topped with marinara sauce, and garnished with chopped fresh basil.

Nutritional information: (per serving, without marinara sauce) 350 calories, 25g protein, 20g carbohydrates, 18g fat, 1g fiber, 220mg cholesterol, 400mg sodium, 350mg potassium

Sous Vide Scallops with Brown Butter Sauce

Yield: 4 servings | Prep time: 15 minutes | Cook time: 45 minutes
Ingredients:

- 1 pound large sea scallops
- Salt and pepper to taste
- 2 tablespoons olive oil
- 4 tablespoons unsalted butter
- 2 cloves garlic, minced
- 1 tablespoon lemon juice
- 1 tablespoon chopped fresh parsley
- Lemon wedges, for serving

Directions:

1. Preheat the sous vide water bath to 122°F (50°C) for medium-rare scallops or 140°F (60°C) for fully cooked scallops.
2. Pat the scallops dry with paper towels and season them generously with salt and pepper.
3. Place the seasoned scallops in a single layer in a vacuum-sealed bag. Drizzle with olive oil. Seal the bag.
4. Submerge the sealed bag in the preheated water bath and cook for 45 minutes.
5. About 10 minutes before the scallops are done cooking, prepare the brown butter sauce. In a skillet over medium heat, melt the unsalted butter.
6. Cook the butter until it turns golden brown and develops a nutty aroma, stirring occasionally, about 5-7 minutes.
7. Add the minced garlic to the brown butter and cook for an additional 1-2 minutes until fragrant.
8. Remove the skillet from the heat and stir in the lemon juice and chopped fresh parsley.
9. Once the scallops are done cooking, carefully remove them from the sous vide bag and pat dry with paper towels.
10. Heat a skillet over high heat. Sear the scallops for 1-2 minutes on each side until golden brown and caramelized.
11. Serve the sous vide scallops hot, drizzled with brown butter sauce, and garnished with lemon wedges.

Nutritional information: (per serving) 300 calories, 20g protein, 2g carbohydrates, 25g fat, 0g fiber, 80mg cholesterol, 450mg sodium, 350mg potassium

Sous Vide Scallops with Champagne Sauce

Yield: 4 servings | Prep time: 15 minutes | Cook time: 1 hour
Ingredients:

- 1 pound large sea scallops
- Salt and pepper to taste
- 2 tablespoons olive oil
- 1/2 cup Champagne or sparkling wine
- 1/4 cup heavy cream
- 2 tablespoons unsalted butter
- 2 shallots, finely chopped
- 2 cloves garlic, minced
- 1 tablespoon chopped fresh parsley
- Lemon wedges, for serving

Directions:

1. Preheat the sous vide water bath to 122°F (50°C) for medium-rare scallops or 140°F (60°C) for fully cooked scallops.
2. Pat the scallops dry with paper towels and season them generously with salt and pepper.
3. Place the seasoned scallops in a single layer in a vacuum-sealed bag. Drizzle with olive oil. Seal the bag.
4. Submerge the sealed bag in the preheated water bath and cook for 1 hour.
5. About 10 minutes before the scallops are done cooking, prepare the Champagne sauce. In a skillet over medium heat, melt the unsalted butter.
6. Add the chopped shallots and minced garlic to the skillet. Cook until softened, about 3-4 minutes.
7. Pour in the Champagne or sparkling wine and let it simmer until reduced by half, about 5-7 minutes.
8. Stir in the heavy cream and chopped fresh parsley. Simmer for an additional 3-4 minutes until the sauce has thickened slightly.
9. Once the scallops are done cooking, carefully remove them from the sous vide bag and pat dry with paper towels.
10. Heat a skillet over high heat. Sear the scallops for 1-2 minutes on each side until golden brown and caramelized.
11. Serve the sous vide scallops hot, drizzled with the Champagne sauce, and garnished with lemon wedges.

Nutritional information: (per serving) 320 calories, 20g protein, 5g carbohydrates, 25g fat, 0g fiber, 80mg cholesterol, 300mg sodium, 350mg potassium

Sous Vide Scallops with Cauliflower Puree

Yield: 4 servings | Prep time: 15 minutes | Cook time: 1 hour
Ingredients:

- 1 pound large sea scallops
- Salt and pepper to taste
- 2 tablespoons olive oil
- 1 head cauliflower, cut into florets
- 2 cloves garlic, minced
- 2 tablespoons unsalted butter
- 1/4 cup heavy cream
- Salt and pepper to taste
- Chopped chives, for garnish
- Lemon wedges, for serving

Directions:

1. Preheat the sous vide water bath to 122°F (50°C) for medium-rare scallops or 140°F (60°C) for fully cooked scallops.

2. Pat the scallops dry with paper towels and season them generously with salt and pepper.
3. Place the seasoned scallops in a single layer in a vacuum-sealed bag. Drizzle with olive oil. Seal the bag.
4. In a separate vacuum-sealed bag, place the cauliflower florets along with minced garlic, unsalted butter, heavy cream, salt, and pepper. Seal the bag.
5. Submerge both sealed bags in the preheated water bath and cook for 1 hour.
6. Once the cooking time is up, carefully remove the bags from the water bath.
7. Using a blender or food processor, puree the cooked cauliflower mixture until smooth. Adjust the seasoning with salt and pepper if needed.
8. Heat a skillet over high heat. Sear the scallops for 1-2 minutes on each side until golden brown and caramelized.
9. Serve the sous vide scallops hot, accompanied by a dollop of cauliflower puree. Garnish with chopped chives and lemon wedges on the side.

Nutritional information: (per serving) 280 calories, 20g protein, 8g carbohydrates, 18g fat, 3g fiber, 60mg cholesterol, 400mg sodium, 600mg potassium

Chapter 7 Sides and Vegetables

Sous Vide Garlic Mashed Potatoes

Yield: 4 servings | Prep time: 10 minutes | Cook time: 1 hour
Ingredients:

- 2 pounds potatoes, peeled and cubed
- 4 cloves garlic, minced
- 1/2 cup unsalted butter
- 1/4 cup heavy cream
- Salt and pepper to taste
- Chopped chives, for garnish (optional)

Directions:

1. Preheat the sous vide water bath to 183°F (84°C).
2. Place the cubed potatoes and minced garlic in a vacuum-sealed bag. Add the unsalted butter to the bag. Seal the bag.
3. Submerge the sealed bag in the preheated water bath and cook for 1 hour.
4. Once the potatoes are cooked, carefully remove the bag from the water bath and open it.
5. Transfer the cooked potatoes and garlic to a large bowl. Reserve some of the cooking liquid.
6. Use a potato masher or fork to mash the potatoes until smooth.
7. Gradually add the heavy cream to the mashed potatoes, stirring until desired consistency is reached. If needed, add some of the reserved cooking liquid to adjust consistency.
8. Season the mashed potatoes with salt and pepper to taste.
9. Serve the sous vide garlic mashed potatoes hot, garnished with chopped chives if desired.

Nutritional information: (per serving) Approximately 280 calories, 3g protein, 25g carbohydrates, 20g fat, 2g fiber, 55mg cholesterol, 20mg sodium, 600mg potassium.

Sous Vide Green Beans with Almonds

Yield: 4 servings | Prep time: 10 minutes | Cook time: 1 hour
Ingredients:

- 1 pound green beans, ends trimmed
- 1/4 cup sliced almonds
- 2 tablespoons olive oil
- 2 cloves garlic, minced
- Salt and pepper to taste
- Lemon wedges, for serving

Directions:

1. Preheat the sous vide water bath to 183°F (84°C).
2. Place the trimmed green beans in a vacuum-sealed bag. Add the sliced almonds, olive oil, minced garlic, salt, and pepper. Seal the bag.
3. Submerge the sealed bag in the preheated water bath and cook for 1 hour.
4. Once the green beans are cooked, carefully remove the bag from the water bath and open it.

5. Drain any excess liquid from the bag.
6. Heat a skillet over medium heat. Add the cooked green beans and almonds to the skillet.
7. Saute the green beans and almonds for 2-3 minutes, stirring occasionally, until heated through and slightly browned.
8. Season with additional salt and pepper if needed.
9. Serve the sous vide green beans with almonds hot, garnished with lemon wedges on the side.

Nutritional information: (per serving) Approximately 120 calories, 3g protein, 7g carbohydrates, 10g fat, 4g fiber, 0mg cholesterol, 10mg sodium, 300mg potassium.

Sous Vide Honey Glazed Carrots

Yield: 4 servings | Prep time: 10 minutes | Cook time: 1 hour
Ingredients:

- 1 pound carrots, peeled and sliced into 1-inch pieces
- 2 tablespoons honey
- 2 tablespoons unsalted butter
- 1 tablespoon fresh thyme leaves
- Salt and pepper to taste

Directions:

1. Preheat the sous vide water bath to 183°F (84°C).
2. Place the sliced carrots in a vacuum-sealed bag. Add the honey, unsalted butter, fresh thyme leaves, salt, and pepper. Seal the bag.
3. Submerge the sealed bag in the preheated water bath and cook for 1 hour.
4. Once the carrots are cooked, carefully remove the bag from the water bath and open it.
5. Heat a skillet over medium heat. Transfer the cooked carrots along with the honey glaze from the bag to the skillet.
6. Saute the carrots for 2-3 minutes, stirring occasionally, until they are evenly coated in the honey glaze and slightly caramelized.
7. Season with additional salt and pepper if needed.
8. Serve the sous vide honey-glazed carrots hot as a side dish.

Nutritional information: (per serving) Approximately 120 calories, 1g protein, 20g carbohydrates, 6g fat, 4g fiber, 15mg cholesterol, 70mg sodium, 400mg potassium.

Sous Vide Asparagus with Lemon Butter

Yield: 4 servings | Prep time: 10 minutes | Cook time: 30 minutes
Ingredients:

- 1 pound asparagus, tough ends trimmed
- 4 tablespoons unsalted butter
- 2 tablespoons fresh lemon juice
- Zest of 1 lemon
- Salt and pepper to taste

Directions:

1. Preheat the sous vide water bath to 185°F (85°C).
2. Divide the trimmed asparagus into serving-sized bundles and place them in separate vacuum-sealed bags.

3. In each bag, add 1 tablespoon of unsalted butter, 1/2 tablespoon of fresh lemon juice, and a pinch of lemon zest. Season with salt and pepper to taste. Seal the bags.
4. Submerge the sealed bags in the preheated water bath and cook for 30 minutes.
5. Once the asparagus is cooked, carefully remove the bags from the water bath and open them.
6. Transfer the cooked asparagus to a serving dish and drizzle with the lemon butter sauce from the bags.
7. Serve the sous vide asparagus with lemon butter hot as a side dish.

Nutritional information: (per serving) Approximately 110 calories, 2g protein, 6g carbohydrates, 9g fat, 3g fiber, 25mg cholesterol, 5mg sodium, 400mg potassium.

Sous Vide Roasted Brussels Sprouts

Yield: 4 servings | Prep time: 10 minutes | Cook time: 1 hour
Ingredients:

- 1 pound Brussels sprouts, trimmed and halved
- 2 tablespoons olive oil
- 4 cloves garlic, minced
- Salt and pepper to taste
- Optional: Balsamic glaze, for drizzling

Directions:

1. Preheat the sous vide water bath to 185°F (85°C).
2. Place the halved Brussels sprouts in a vacuum-sealed bag. Add the olive oil, minced garlic, salt, and pepper. Seal the bag.
3. Submerge the sealed bag in the preheated water bath and cook for 1 hour.
4. Once the Brussels sprouts are cooked, carefully remove the bag from the water bath and open it.
5. Heat a skillet over medium-high heat. Transfer the cooked Brussels sprouts to the skillet, reserving the garlic-infused olive oil.
6. Saute the Brussels sprouts in the skillet for 3-4 minutes, stirring occasionally, until they are lightly browned and caramelized.
7. Drizzle the reserved garlic-infused olive oil over the Brussels sprouts and toss to coat evenly.
8. Serve the sous vide roasted Brussels sprouts hot as a side dish. Optionally, drizzle with balsamic glaze before serving.

Nutritional information: (per serving) Approximately 120 calories, 4g protein, 10g carbohydrates, 8g fat, 4g fiber, 0mg cholesterol, 20mg sodium, 450mg potassium.

Sous Vide Creamed Spinach

Yield: 4 servings | Prep time: 10 minutes | Cook time: 1 hour
Ingredients:

- 1 pound fresh spinach, washed and trimmed
- 2 tablespoons unsalted butter
- 2 cloves garlic, minced
- 1/4 cup heavy cream
- 1/4 cup grated Parmesan cheese
- Salt and pepper to taste
- Pinch of nutmeg (optional)

Directions:

1. Preheat the sous vide water bath to 183°F (84°C).
2. Place the washed and trimmed spinach in a vacuum-sealed bag. Add the unsalted butter and minced garlic. Seal the bag.
3. Submerge the sealed bag in the preheated water bath and cook for 1 hour.
4. Once the spinach is cooked, carefully remove the bag from the water bath and open it.
5. Transfer the cooked spinach to a colander and drain any excess liquid.
6. In a skillet over medium heat, combine the cooked spinach, heavy cream, and grated Parmesan cheese. Stir until the cheese is melted and the cream is heated through.
7. Season the creamed spinach with salt, pepper, and a pinch of nutmeg if desired.
8. Serve the sous vide creamed spinach hot as a side dish.

Nutritional information: (per serving) Approximately 150 calories, 6g protein, 5g carbohydrates, 12g fat, 3g fiber, 35mg cholesterol, 250mg sodium, 900mg potassium.

Sous Vide Glazed Baby Carrots

Yield: 4 servings | Prep time: 10 minutes | Cook time: 1 hour
Ingredients:

- 1 pound baby carrots, peeled
- 2 tablespoons unsalted butter
- 2 tablespoons honey
- 1 tablespoon brown sugar
- 1/4 teaspoon ground cinnamon
- Salt and pepper to taste
- Chopped parsley, for garnish (optional)

Directions:

1. Preheat the sous vide water bath to 183°F (84°C).
2. Place the peeled baby carrots in a vacuum-sealed bag. Add the unsalted butter, honey, brown sugar, ground cinnamon, salt, and pepper. Seal the bag.
3. Submerge the sealed bag in the preheated water bath and cook for 1 hour.
4. Once the carrots are cooked, carefully remove the bag from the water bath and open it.
5. Heat a skillet over medium heat. Transfer the cooked carrots along with the glaze from the bag to the skillet.
6. Saute the carrots in the skillet for 2-3 minutes, stirring occasionally, until the glaze thickens and coats the carrots.
7. Season with additional salt and pepper if needed.
8. Serve the sous vide glazed baby carrots hot as a side dish, garnished with chopped parsley if desired.

Nutritional information: (per serving) Approximately 150 calories, 1g protein, 25g carbohydrates, 7g fat, 4g fiber, 20mg cholesterol, 100mg sodium, 400mg potassium.

Sous Vide Corn on the Cob with Garlic Herb Butter

Yield: 4 servings | Prep time: 10 minutes | Cook time: 1 hour
Ingredients:

- 4 ears of corn, husked and cleaned
- 4 tablespoons unsalted butter
- 2 cloves garlic, minced
- 1 tablespoon fresh herbs (such as parsley, thyme, or basil), chopped

- Salt and pepper to taste

Directions:

1. Preheat the sous vide water bath to 183°F (84°C).
2. Divide the cleaned ears of corn into individual vacuum-sealed bags, one ear per bag.
3. In a small bowl, combine the unsalted butter, minced garlic, chopped fresh herbs, salt, and pepper.
4. Place 1 tablespoon of the garlic herb butter mixture into each bag with the corn.
5. Seal the bags.
6. Submerge the sealed bags in the preheated water bath and cook for 1 hour.
7. Once the corn is cooked, carefully remove the bags from the water bath and open them.
8. Transfer the cooked corn to a serving platter or individual plates.
9. Serve the sous vide corn on the cob hot, with any remaining garlic herb butter drizzled over the top.

Nutritional information: (per serving) Approximately 180 calories, 3g protein, 22g carbohydrates, 11g fat, 3g fiber, 30mg cholesterol, 0mg sodium, 300mg potassium.

Sous Vide Sweet Potato Mash

Yield: 4 servings | Prep time: 10 minutes | Cook time: 1 hour

Ingredients:

- 2 large sweet potatoes, peeled and cubed
- 2 tablespoons unsalted butter
- 1/4 cup milk (or dairy-free alternative)
- 1 tablespoon maple syrup (optional)
- Salt and pepper to taste
- Chopped chives or parsley, for garnish (optional)

Directions:

1. Preheat the sous vide water bath to 183°F (84°C).
2. Place the cubed sweet potatoes in a vacuum-sealed bag. Add the unsalted butter and season with salt and pepper. Seal the bag.
3. Submerge the sealed bag in the preheated water bath and cook for 1 hour.
4. Once the sweet potatoes are cooked, carefully remove the bag from the water bath and open it.
5. Transfer the cooked sweet potatoes to a large bowl. Use a potato masher or fork to mash the sweet potatoes until smooth.
6. Gradually add the milk (or dairy-free alternative) to the mashed sweet potatoes, stirring until the desired consistency is reached.
7. Optionally, add maple syrup for sweetness and adjust seasoning with salt and pepper if needed.
8. Serve the sous vide sweet potato mash hot, garnished with chopped chives or parsley if desired.

Nutritional information: (per serving) Approximately 150 calories, 2g protein, 25g carbohydrates, 6g fat, 4g fiber, 15mg cholesterol, 50mg sodium, 400mg potassium.

Sous Vide Roasted Root Vegetables

Yield: 4 servings | Prep time: 15 minutes | Cook time: 1 hour

Ingredients:

- 2 large carrots, peeled and cut into chunks
- 2 parsnips, peeled and cut into chunks

- 2 turnips, peeled and cut into chunks
- 2 beets, peeled and cut into chunks
- 2 tablespoons olive oil
- 2 cloves garlic, minced
- 1 teaspoon dried thyme
- Salt and pepper to taste
- Chopped fresh parsley, for garnish (optional)

Directions:

1. Preheat the sous vide water bath to 183°F (84°C).
2. Place the cut carrots, parsnips, turnips, and beets in a large bowl. Add the olive oil, minced garlic, dried thyme, salt, and pepper. Toss until the vegetables are evenly coated.
3. Divide the seasoned vegetables into individual vacuum-sealed bags, ensuring an even distribution of vegetables in each bag.
4. Seal the bags.
5. Submerge the sealed bags in the preheated water bath and cook for 1 hour.
6. Once the vegetables are cooked, carefully remove the bags from the water bath and open them.
7. Preheat the oven broiler to high.
8. Transfer the cooked vegetables to a baking sheet lined with parchment paper.
9. Place the baking sheet under the broiler and broil for 3-5 minutes, or until the vegetables are lightly browned and caramelized.
10. Remove the baking sheet from the oven and transfer the roasted root vegetables to a serving dish.
11. Garnish with chopped fresh parsley if desired.
12. Serve the sous vide roasted root vegetables hot as a side dish.

Nutritional information: (per serving) Approximately 150 calories, 2g protein, 20g carbohydrates, 7g fat, 5g fiber, 0mg cholesterol, 200mg sodium, 600mg potassium.

Sous Vide Herbed Rice Pilaf

Yield: 4 servings | Prep time: 10 minutes | Cook time: 1 hour

Ingredients:

- 1 cup long-grain white rice
- 2 cups vegetable broth
- 2 tablespoons unsalted butter
- 2 cloves garlic, minced
- 1/4 cup finely chopped onion
- 1 teaspoon dried thyme
- 1 teaspoon dried parsley
- Salt and pepper to taste
- Chopped fresh parsley, for garnish (optional)

Directions:

1. Preheat the sous vide water bath to 185°F (85°C).
2. In a large bowl, combine the white rice and vegetable broth. Stir well to ensure the rice is evenly coated.
3. Divide the rice mixture into individual vacuum-sealed bags, ensuring an even distribution of rice in each bag.
4. Seal the bags, removing as much air as possible.
5. Submerge the sealed bags in the preheated water bath and cook for 1 hour.
6. Once the rice is cooked, carefully remove the bags from the water bath and open them.

7. In a skillet over medium heat, melt the unsalted butter. Add the minced garlic and finely chopped onion. Saute until the onion is translucent and fragrant, about 3-4 minutes.
8. Add the cooked rice to the skillet with the garlic and onion mixture. Stir in the dried thyme and dried parsley. Season with salt and pepper to taste.
9. Cook the rice pilaf, stirring occasionally, for an additional 3-5 minutes, allowing the flavors to meld together.
10. Garnish with chopped fresh parsley before serving, if desired.
11. Serve the sous vide herbed rice pilaf hot as a side dish.

Nutritional information: (per serving) Approximately 200 calories, 3g protein, 35g carbohydrates, 6g fat, 2g fiber, 15mg cholesterol, 600mg sodium, 100mg potassium.

Sous Vide Honey Balsamic Glazed Brussels Sprouts

Yield: 4 servings | Prep time: 10 minutes | Cook time: 1 hour
Ingredients:

- 1 pound Brussels sprouts, trimmed and halved
- 2 tablespoons olive oil
- 2 tablespoons balsamic vinegar
- 2 tablespoons honey
- 2 cloves garlic, minced
- Salt and pepper to taste
- Chopped fresh parsley, for garnish (optional)

Directions:

1. Preheat the sous vide water bath to 183°F (84°C).
2. In a bowl, whisk together the olive oil, balsamic vinegar, honey, minced garlic, salt, and pepper.
3. Place the trimmed and halved Brussels sprouts in a vacuum-sealed bag. Pour the honey balsamic mixture over the Brussels sprouts.
4. Seal the bag, removing as much air as possible.
5. Submerge the sealed bag in the preheated water bath and cook for 1 hour.
6. Once the Brussels sprouts are cooked, carefully remove the bag from the water bath and open it.
7. Preheat the oven broiler to high.
8. Transfer the cooked Brussels sprouts to a baking sheet lined with parchment paper.
9. Place the baking sheet under the broiler and broil for 3-5 minutes, or until the Brussels sprouts are caramelized and slightly charred.
10. Remove the baking sheet from the oven and transfer the Brussels sprouts to a serving dish.
11. Garnish with chopped fresh parsley, if desired.
12. Serve the sous vide honey balsamic glazed Brussels sprouts hot as a side dish.

Nutritional information: (per serving) Approximately 120 calories, 3g protein, 20g carbohydrates, 4g fat, 5g fiber, 0mg cholesterol, 50mg sodium, 500mg potassium.

Sous Vide Lemon Garlic Broccoli

Yield: 4 servings | Prep time: 10 minutes | Cook time: 1 hour
Ingredients:

- 1 pound broccoli florets
- 2 tablespoons olive oil
- 2 cloves garlic, minced

- Zest of 1 lemon
- Juice of 1 lemon
- Salt and pepper to taste
- Crushed red pepper flakes (optional)
- Grated Parmesan cheese, for garnish (optional)

Directions:

1. Preheat the sous vide water bath to 183°F (84°C).
2. In a bowl, mix the olive oil, minced garlic, lemon zest, lemon juice, salt, pepper, and optional crushed red pepper flakes.
3. Place the broccoli florets in a vacuum-sealed bag. Pour the lemon garlic mixture over the broccoli.
4. Seal the bag, removing as much air as possible.
5. Submerge the sealed bag in the preheated water bath and cook for 1 hour.
6. Once the broccoli is cooked, carefully remove the bag from the water bath and open it.
7. Preheat a skillet over medium-high heat.
8. Transfer the cooked broccoli to the skillet, allowing any excess liquid to evaporate.
9. Sauté the broccoli for 2-3 minutes, until lightly browned and crisp-tender.
10. Transfer the cooked broccoli to a serving dish.
11. Garnish with grated Parmesan cheese, if desired.
12. Serve the sous vide lemon garlic broccoli hot as a side dish.

Nutritional information: (per serving) Approximately 90 calories, 3g protein, 8g carbohydrates, 6g fat, 3g fiber, 0mg cholesterol, 70mg sodium, 400mg potassium.

Sous Vide Parmesan Zucchini

Yield: 4 servings | Prep time: 10 minutes | Cook time: 1 hour
Ingredients:

- 2 medium zucchinis, sliced into rounds
- 2 tablespoons olive oil
- 1/4 cup grated Parmesan cheese
- 2 cloves garlic, minced
- 1 teaspoon dried oregano
- Salt and pepper to taste
- Chopped fresh parsley, for garnish (optional)

Directions:

1. Preheat the sous vide water bath to 183°F (84°C).
2. In a bowl, combine the olive oil, grated Parmesan cheese, minced garlic, dried oregano, salt, and pepper.
3. Place the sliced zucchini in a vacuum-sealed bag. Pour the Parmesan mixture over the zucchini.
4. Seal the bag, removing as much air as possible.
5. Submerge the sealed bag in the preheated water bath and cook for 1 hour.
6. Once the zucchinis are cooked, carefully remove the bag from the water bath and open it.
7. Preheat a skillet over medium-high heat.
8. Transfer the cooked zucchini to the skillet, allowing any excess liquid to evaporate.
9. Sauté the zucchinis for 2-3 minutes, until lightly browned and tender.
10. Transfer the cooked zucchini to a serving dish.
11. Garnish with chopped fresh parsley, if desired.
12. Serve the sous vide Parmesan zucchini hot as a side dish.

Nutritional information: (per serving) Approximately 110 calories, 3g protein, 6g carbohydrates, 9g fat, 2g fiber, 5mg cholesterol, 150mg sodium, 400mg potassium.

Sous Vide Butternut Squash Puree

Yield: 4 servings | Prep time: 10 minutes | Cook time: 1 hour

Ingredients:

- 1 medium butternut squash, peeled, seeded, and diced
- 2 tablespoons unsalted butter
- 2 cloves garlic, minced
- 1/4 cup heavy cream
- Salt and pepper to taste
- Pinch of ground nutmeg (optional)
- Chopped fresh parsley, for garnish (optional)

Directions:

1. Preheat the sous vide water bath to 185°F (85°C).
2. Place the diced butternut squash in a vacuum-sealed bag along with the unsalted butter and minced garlic.
3. Seal the bag, removing as much air as possible.
4. Submerge the sealed bag in the preheated water bath and cook for 1 hour.
5. Once the butternut squash is cooked, carefully remove the bag from the water bath and open it.
6. Transfer the cooked butternut squash to a blender or food processor.
7. Add the heavy cream, salt, pepper, and optional ground nutmeg to the blender.
8. Blend until smooth and creamy, adding more cream if needed to reach the desired consistency.
9. Taste and adjust seasoning, if necessary.
10. Transfer the butternut squash puree to a serving bowl.
11. Garnish with chopped fresh parsley, if desired, before serving.
12. Serve the sous vide butternut squash puree hot as a side dish.

Nutritional information: (per serving) Approximately 120 calories, 1g protein, 15g carbohydrates, 7g fat, 3g fiber, 20mg cholesterol, 50mg sodium, 600mg potassium.

Chapter 8 Sous Vide for Vegetarian and Vegan recipes

Sous Vide Ratatouille

Yield: 4 servings | Prep time: 20 minutes | Cook time: 2 hours

Ingredients:

- 1 large eggplant, diced
- 2 medium zucchinis, diced
- 1 large red bell pepper, diced
- 1 large yellow bell pepper, diced
- 1 onion, diced
- 3 cloves garlic, minced
- 4 tomatoes, diced
- 2 tablespoons olive oil
- 1 tablespoon balsamic vinegar
- 1 teaspoon dried thyme
- 1 teaspoon dried oregano
- Salt and pepper to taste

Directions:

1. Preheat the sous vide water bath to 185°F (85°C).
2. In a large bowl, toss together the diced eggplant, zucchinis, red and yellow bell peppers, onion, garlic, tomatoes, olive oil, balsamic vinegar, dried thyme, dried oregano, salt, and pepper until well combined.
3. Divide the mixture evenly among vacuum-sealable bags, ensuring each bag has an equal mix of vegetables.
4. Seal the bags using a vacuum sealer, ensuring all the air is removed.
5. Place the sealed bags in the preheated water bath and cook for 2 hours.
6. Once cooked, carefully remove the bags from the water bath and let them cool slightly before opening.
7. Serve the ratatouille warm, garnished with fresh herbs if desired.

Nutritional information: Approximately 180 calories, 4g protein, 22g carbohydrates, 9g fat, 8g fiber, 0mg cholesterol, 350mg sodium, 900mg potassium

Sous Vide Cauliflower Steaks with Chimichurri Sauce

Yield: 4 servings | Prep time: 15 minutes | Cook time: 1 hour

Ingredients:

- 1 large head of cauliflower
- 2 tablespoons olive oil
- Salt and pepper to taste

For the Chimichurri Sauce:

- 1 cup fresh parsley, chopped

- 1/4 cup fresh cilantro, chopped
- 3 cloves garlic, minced
- 1 shallot, finely chopped
- 1/4 cup red wine vinegar
- 1/2 cup olive oil
- 1 teaspoon dried oregano
- Salt and pepper to taste
- Red pepper flakes (optional)

Directions:

1. Preheat the sous vide water bath to 185°F (85°C).
2. Remove the leaves from the cauliflower and trim the stem end to create a flat base. Slice the cauliflower into 1-inch thick steaks.
3. Brush both sides of each cauliflower steak with olive oil and season with salt and pepper.
4. Place the cauliflower steaks in a single layer in a vacuum-sealable bag, ensuring they are not overlapping.
5. Seal the bag using a vacuum sealer, removing all the air.
6. Once the water bath is ready, submerge the bag in the water bath and cook for 1 hour.
7. While the cauliflower is cooking, prepare the chimichurri sauce. In a bowl, combine the chopped parsley, cilantro, garlic, shallot, red wine vinegar, olive oil, dried oregano, salt, pepper, and red pepper flakes if using. Mix well to combine.
8. Once the cauliflower is cooked, carefully remove the bag from the water bath and open it.
9. Heat a grill or grill pan over medium-high heat. Remove the cauliflower steaks from the bag and grill for 2-3 minutes on each side, or until lightly charred.
10. Serve the grilled cauliflower steaks with chimichurri sauce drizzled on top.

Nutritional information: Approximately 180 calories, 3g protein, 10g carbohydrates, 15g fat, 4g fiber, 0mg cholesterol, 350mg sodium, 550mg potassium.

Sous Vide Eggplant Parmesan

Yield: 4 servings | Prep time: 20 minutes | Cook time: 1 hour
Ingredients:

- 2 large eggplants, sliced into 1/2-inch rounds
- Salt
- 2 cups marinara sauce
- 1 cup breadcrumbs
- 1 cup grated Parmesan cheese
- 2 eggs, beaten
- 1 cup shredded mozzarella cheese
- Fresh basil leaves, for garnish

Directions:

1. Preheat the sous vide water bath to 185°F (85°C).
2. Sprinkle the eggplant slices with salt and let them sit for 10 minutes to draw out excess moisture. Pat them dry with paper towels.
3. In a shallow dish, combine the breadcrumbs and grated Parmesan cheese.
4. Dip each eggplant slice into the beaten eggs, then coat them with the breadcrumb mixture, pressing gently to adhere.

5. Place the breaded eggplant slices in a single layer in vacuum-sealable bags, making sure they are not overlapping.
6. Seal the bags using a vacuum sealer, ensuring all the air is removed.
7. Once the water bath is ready, submerge the bags in the water bath and cook for 1 hour.
8. Preheat the oven to 375°F (190°C).
9. Remove the cooked eggplant slices from the bags and arrange them in a baking dish.
10. Pour marinara sauce over the eggplant slices and sprinkle shredded mozzarella cheese on top.
11. Bake in the preheated oven for 20-25 minutes, or until the cheese is melted and bubbly.
12. Garnish with fresh basil leaves before serving.

Nutritional information: Approximately 280 calories, 14g protein, 30g carbohydrates, 12g fat, 6g fiber, 95mg cholesterol, 950mg sodium, 800mg potassium.

Sous Vide Stuffed Bell Peppers with Quinoa and Vegetables

Yield: 4 servings | Prep time: 25 minutes | Cook time: 1 hour
Ingredients:

- 4 large bell peppers, any color
- 1 cup quinoa, rinsed
- 2 cups vegetable broth
- 1 tablespoon olive oil
- 1 onion, diced
- 2 cloves garlic, minced
- 1 zucchini, diced
- 1 carrot, diced
- 1 cup diced tomatoes
- 1 teaspoon dried oregano
- 1 teaspoon dried basil
- Salt and pepper to taste
- 1 cup shredded mozzarella cheese (optional)

Directions:

1. Preheat the sous vide water bath to 185°F (85°C).
2. Cut the tops off the bell peppers and remove the seeds and membranes. Set aside.
3. In a saucepan, combine the quinoa and vegetable broth. Bring to a boil, then reduce the heat to low, cover, and simmer for 15 minutes or until the quinoa is cooked and the liquid is absorbed.
4. In a skillet, heat olive oil over medium heat. Add the diced onion and cook until softened about 5 minutes. Add the minced garlic and cook for an additional minute.
5. Add the diced zucchini, carrot, diced tomatoes, dried oregano, dried basil, salt, and pepper to the skillet. Cook for 5-7 minutes, or until the vegetables are tender.
6. In a large bowl, combine the cooked quinoa and cooked vegetable mixture.
7. Stuff each bell pepper with the quinoa and vegetable mixture, pressing down gently to pack it in.
8. Place the stuffed bell peppers in vacuum-sealable bags, ensuring they are standing upright.
9. Seal the bags using a vacuum sealer, ensuring all the air is removed.
10. Once the water bath is ready, submerge the bags in the water bath and cook for 1 hour.
11. Carefully remove the stuffed bell peppers from the bags and serve hot. Optionally, sprinkle shredded mozzarella cheese on top before serving.

Nutritional information: Approximately 280 calories, 10g protein, 45g carbohydrates, 8g fat, 8g fiber, 0mg cholesterol, 600mg sodium, 800mg potassium.

Sous Vide Portobello Mushrooms with Balsamic Glaze

Yield: 4 servings | Prep time: 10 minutes | Cook time: 1 hour

Ingredients:

- 4 large portobello mushrooms
- 2 tablespoons balsamic vinegar
- 2 tablespoons olive oil
- 2 cloves garlic, minced
- 1 teaspoon dried thyme
- Salt and pepper to taste
- Fresh parsley, for garnish

For the Balsamic Glaze:

- 1/2 cup balsamic vinegar
- 2 tablespoons honey or maple syrup

Directions:

1. Preheat the sous vide water bath to 175°F (80°C).
2. Clean the portobello mushrooms and remove the stems.
3. In a small bowl, whisk together the balsamic vinegar, olive oil, minced garlic, dried thyme, salt, and pepper.
4. Place the portobello mushrooms in a single layer in vacuum-sealable bags.
5. Pour the balsamic vinegar mixture over the mushrooms, ensuring they are well coated.
6. Seal the bags using a vacuum sealer, ensuring all the air is removed.
7. Once the water bath is ready, submerge the bags in the water bath and cook for 1 hour.
8. While the mushrooms are cooking, prepare the balsamic glaze. In a small saucepan, combine the balsamic vinegar and honey or maple syrup. Bring to a simmer over medium heat and cook for 10-15 minutes, or until the glaze has thickened slightly. Remove from heat and set aside.
9. After 1 hour, carefully remove the bags from the water bath and open them.
10. Heat a grill or grill pan over medium-high heat. Remove the mushrooms from the bags and grill for 2-3 minutes on each side or until tender and slightly charred.
11. Serve the grilled portobello mushrooms drizzled with the balsamic glaze and garnished with fresh parsley.

Nutritional information: Approximately 120 calories, 4g protein, 10g carbohydrates, 8g fat, 2g fiber, 0mg cholesterol, 10mg sodium, 500mg potassium.

Sous Vide Sweet Potato Hash

Yield: 4 servings | Prep time: 15 minutes | Cook time: 1 hour

Ingredients:

- 2 large sweet potatoes, peeled and diced
- 1 onion, diced
- 1 red bell pepper, diced
- 2 cloves garlic, minced
- 2 tablespoons olive oil
- 1 teaspoon smoked paprika
- 1/2 teaspoon ground cumin
- Salt and pepper to taste

- Fresh parsley or cilantro, for garnish

Directions:

1. Preheat the sous vide water bath to 185°F (85°C).
2. In a large bowl, toss together the diced sweet potatoes, onion, red bell pepper, minced garlic, olive oil, smoked paprika, ground cumin, salt, and pepper until well combined.
3. Divide the sweet potato mixture evenly among vacuum-sealable bags.
4. Seal the bags using a vacuum sealer, ensuring all the air is removed.
5. Once the water bath is ready, submerge the bags in the water bath and cook for 1 hour.
6. After 1 hour, carefully remove the bags from the water bath and open them.
7. Heat a skillet over medium-high heat. Remove the sweet potato mixture from the bags and transfer it to the skillet.
8. Cook the sweet potato hash in the skillet, stirring occasionally, until the sweet potatoes are tender and lightly browned, about 5-7 minutes.
9. Serve the sweet potato hash hot, garnished with fresh parsley or cilantro if desired.

Nutritional information: Approximately 180 calories, 2g protein, 25g carbohydrates, 9g fat, 4g fiber, 0mg cholesterol, 150mg sodium, 550mg potassium.

Sous Vide Carrot Ginger Soup

Yield: 4 servings | Prep time: 10 minutes | Cook time: 1 hour

Ingredients:

- 1 lb (450g) carrots, peeled and chopped
- 1 onion, chopped
- 2 cloves garlic, minced
- 1 tablespoon fresh ginger, grated
- 4 cups (1 liter) vegetable broth
- 2 tablespoons olive oil
- Salt and pepper to taste
- Fresh cilantro or parsley, for garnish (optional)

Directions:

1. Preheat the sous vide water bath to 185°F (85°C).
2. Place the chopped carrots, onion, minced garlic, and grated ginger in a large vacuum-sealable bag.
3. Add the vegetable broth, olive oil, salt, and pepper to the bag.
4. Seal the bag using a vacuum sealer, ensuring all the air is removed.
5. Once the water bath is ready, submerge the bag in the water bath and cook for 1 hour.
6. After 1 hour, carefully remove the bag from the water bath and open it.
7. Using an immersion blender or regular blender, blend the soup until smooth.
8. If necessary, adjust the seasoning with additional salt and pepper to taste.
9. Serve the carrot ginger soup hot, garnished with fresh cilantro or parsley if desired.

Nutritional information: Approximately 120 calories, 2g protein, 15g carbohydrates, 7g fat, 4g fiber, 0mg cholesterol, 1000mg sodium, 550mg potassium.

Sous Vide Vegan Risotto with Mushrooms

Yield: 4 servings | Prep time: 15 minutes | Cook time: 1 hour

Ingredients:

- 1 cup Arborio rice
- 4 cups vegetable broth
- 1 tablespoon olive oil
- 1 onion, finely chopped
- 2 cloves garlic, minced
- 8 oz (225g) mushrooms, sliced
- 1/2 cup white wine (optional)
- 1/4 cup nutritional yeast
- Salt and pepper to taste
- Fresh parsley, chopped, for garnish

Directions:

1. Preheat the sous vide water bath to 185°F (85°C).
2. In a large vacuum-sealable bag, combine the Arborio rice and vegetable broth.
3. Seal the bag using a vacuum sealer, ensuring all the air is removed.
4. Once the water bath is ready, submerge the bag in the water bath and cook for 1 hour.
5. About 20 minutes before the risotto is done cooking, heat olive oil in a skillet over medium heat.
6. Add the chopped onion and minced garlic to the skillet and sauté until softened, about 5 minutes.
7. Add the sliced mushrooms to the skillet and cook until they release their moisture and become tender, about 7-10 minutes.
8. If using, pour in the white wine and simmer until it has evaporated.
9. Once the sous vide cooking is complete, carefully remove the bag from the water bath and open it.
10. Pour the cooked rice and broth into a large bowl. Stir in the sautéed mushrooms, nutritional yeast, salt, and pepper.
11. Serve the vegan risotto hot, garnished with fresh chopped parsley.

Nutritional information: Approximately 250 calories, 6g protein, 45g carbohydrates, 5g fat, 3g fiber, 0mg cholesterol, 1200mg sodium, 300mg potassium.

Sous Vide Tofu Scramble

Yield: 4 servings | Prep time: 10 minutes | Cook time: 1 hour

Ingredients:

- 1 block (14 oz / 400g) firm tofu, drained and pressed
- 2 tablespoons olive oil
- 1 onion, diced
- 1 bell pepper, diced
- 2 cloves garlic, minced
- 1 teaspoon ground turmeric
- 1/2 teaspoon ground cumin
- Salt and pepper to taste
- Fresh cilantro or parsley, for garnish (optional)

Directions:

1. Preheat the sous vide water bath to 160°F (71°C).
2. Crumble the drained and pressed tofu into a large mixing bowl.
3. Heat olive oil in a skillet over medium heat. Add diced onion, bell pepper, and minced garlic. Sauté until softened, about 5 minutes.

4. Add the sautéed vegetables to the crumbled tofu in the mixing bowl.
5. Add ground turmeric, ground cumin, salt, and pepper to the bowl. Mix well to combine.
6. Transfer the seasoned tofu mixture into a vacuum-sealable bag, spreading it out evenly.
7. Seal the bag using a vacuum sealer, ensuring all the air is removed.
8. Once the water bath is ready, submerge the bag in the water bath and cook for 1 hour.
9. After 1 hour, carefully remove the bag from the water bath and open it.
10. Serve the tofu scramble hot, garnished with fresh cilantro or parsley if desired.

Nutritional information: Approximately 180 calories, 12g protein, 8g carbohydrates, 12g fat, 3g fiber, 0mg cholesterol, 300mg sodium, 500mg potassium.

Sous Vide Vegetable Curry

Yield: 4 servings | Prep time: 15 minutes | Cook time: 1 hour
Ingredients:

- 2 cups mixed vegetables (such as carrots, bell peppers, peas, cauliflower, and green beans), chopped
- 1 onion, diced
- 2 cloves garlic, minced
- 1 tablespoon fresh ginger, grated
- 1 can (14 oz / 400ml) coconut milk
- 2 tablespoons curry powder
- 1 teaspoon ground turmeric
- 1 teaspoon ground cumin
- Salt and pepper to taste
- Fresh cilantro, chopped, for garnish
- Cooked rice or naan bread, for serving

Directions:

1. Preheat the sous vide water bath to 185°F (85°C).
2. Place the chopped mixed vegetables, diced onion, minced garlic, and grated ginger in a large vacuum-sealable bag.
3. In a bowl, whisk together the coconut milk, curry powder, ground turmeric, ground cumin, salt, and pepper until well combined.
4. Pour the coconut milk mixture into the bag with the vegetables.
5. Seal the bag using a vacuum sealer, ensuring all the air is removed.
6. Once the water bath is ready, submerge the bag in the water bath and cook for 1 hour.
7. After 1 hour, carefully remove the bag from the water bath and open it.
8. Serve the vegetable curry hot, garnished with fresh chopped cilantro. Serve with cooked rice or naan bread.

Nutritional information: Approximately 250 calories, 5g protein, 15g carbohydrates, 20g fat, 5g fiber, 0mg cholesterol, 300mg sodium, 600mg potassium.

Sous Vide Butternut Squash Risotto

Yield: 4 servings | Prep time: 15 minutes | Cook time: 1 hour
Ingredients:

- 1 small butternut squash, peeled, seeded, and diced
- 2 cups Arborio rice

- 4 cups vegetable broth
- 1 onion, finely chopped
- 2 cloves garlic, minced
- 2 tablespoons olive oil
- 1/2 cup dry white wine (optional)
- 1/2 cup grated Parmesan cheese
- Salt and pepper to taste
- Fresh sage leaves, chopped, for garnish

Directions:

1. Preheat the sous vide water bath to 185°F (85°C).
2. Place the diced butternut squash, Arborio rice, vegetable broth, chopped onion, minced garlic, and olive oil in a large vacuum-sealable bag.
3. Seal the bag using a vacuum sealer, ensuring all the air is removed.
4. Once the water bath is ready, submerge the bag in the water bath and cook for 1 hour.
5. About 20 minutes before the risotto is done cooking, heat a skillet over medium heat. Add the dry white wine (if using) and simmer until reduced by half.
6. After 1 hour, carefully remove the bag from the water bath and open it.
7. Transfer the cooked risotto mixture to the skillet with the reduced white wine.
8. Stir in the grated Parmesan cheese until melted and well combined. Season with salt and pepper to taste.
9. Serve the butternut squash risotto hot, garnished with chopped fresh sage leaves.

Nutritional information: Approximately 350 calories, 8g protein, 60g carbohydrates, 8g fat, 5g fiber, 5mg cholesterol, 900mg sodium, 600mg potassium.

Sous Vide Beetroot Salad with Goat Cheese and Walnuts

Yield: 4 servings | Prep time: 15 minutes | Cook time: 1 hour
Ingredients:

- 4 medium beetroots, peeled and sliced
- 2 tablespoons olive oil
- Salt and pepper to taste
- 4 cups mixed salad greens
- 1/2 cup goat cheese, crumbled
- 1/4 cup walnuts, chopped
- Balsamic glaze, for drizzling

Directions:

1. Preheat the sous vide water bath to 185°F (85°C).
2. Place the sliced beetroots in a bowl and toss with olive oil, salt, and pepper until evenly coated.
3. Transfer the seasoned beetroots to a vacuum-sealable bag, spreading them out evenly.
4. Seal the bag using a vacuum sealer, ensuring all the air is removed.
5. Once the water bath is ready, submerge the bag in the water bath and cook for 1 hour.
6. After 1 hour, carefully remove the bag from the water bath and open it.
7. Divide the mixed salad greens among serving plates.
8. Top the salad greens with the cooked beetroot slices.
9. Sprinkle crumbled goat cheese and chopped walnuts over the salads.
10. Drizzle with balsamic glaze before serving.

Nutritional information: Approximately 180 calories, 5g protein, 15g carbohydrates, 10g fat, 4g fiber, 10mg cholesterol, 200mg sodium, 600mg potassium.

Sous Vide Brussels Sprouts with Maple Glaze

Yield: 4 servings | Prep time: 10 minutes | Cook time: 1 hour

Ingredients:

- 1 lb (450g) Brussels sprouts, trimmed and halved
- 2 tablespoons olive oil
- 2 tablespoons maple syrup
- 1 tablespoon balsamic vinegar
- Salt and pepper to taste
- Optional: chopped pecans or walnuts for garnish

Directions:

1. Preheat the sous vide water bath to 185°F (85°C).
2. In a bowl, whisk together the olive oil, maple syrup, balsamic vinegar, salt, and pepper.
3. Place the halved Brussels sprouts in a vacuum-sealable bag.
4. Pour the maple glaze over the Brussels sprouts in the bag, ensuring they are well coated.
5. Seal the bag using a vacuum sealer, ensuring all the air is removed.
6. Once the water bath is ready, submerge the bag in the water bath and cook for 1 hour.
7. After 1 hour, carefully remove the bag from the water bath and open it.
8. Heat a skillet over medium-high heat. Transfer the cooked Brussels sprouts to the skillet.
9. Sauté the Brussels sprouts in the skillet for a few minutes, stirring occasionally, until caramelized.
10. Serve the sous vide Brussels sprouts hot, garnished with chopped pecans or walnuts if desired.

Nutritional information: Approximately 150 calories, 4g protein, 20g carbohydrates, 8g fat, 6g fiber, 0mg cholesterol, 150mg sodium, 600mg potassium.

Sous Vide Garlic Rosemary Potatoes

Yield: 4 servings | Prep time: 10 minutes | Cook time: 1 hour

Ingredients:

- 1 lb (450g) baby potatoes, halved
- 2 tablespoons olive oil
- 4 cloves garlic, minced
- 2 sprigs of fresh rosemary, chopped
- Salt and pepper to taste
- Optional: grated Parmesan cheese for garnish

Directions:

1. Preheat the sous vide water bath to 185°F (85°C).
2. Place the halved baby potatoes in a bowl.
3. In a separate small bowl, mix the olive oil, minced garlic, chopped rosemary, salt, and pepper.
4. Pour the olive oil mixture over the baby potatoes and toss until well-coated.
5. Transfer the seasoned potatoes to a vacuum-sealable bag, ensuring they are in a single layer.
6. Seal the bag using a vacuum sealer, ensuring all the air is removed.
7. Once the water bath is ready, submerge the bag in the water bath and cook for 1 hour.
8. After 1 hour, carefully remove the bag from the water bath and open it.

9. Heat a skillet over medium-high heat. Transfer the cooked potatoes to the skillet.
10. Sauté the potatoes in the skillet for a few minutes, stirring occasionally, until they are lightly browned and crispy.
11. Serve the sous vide garlic rosemary potatoes hot, garnished with grated Parmesan cheese if desired.

Nutritional information: Approximately 200 calories, 3g protein, 25g carbohydrates, 10g fat, 3g fiber, 0mg cholesterol, 150mg sodium, 600mg potassium.

Sous Vide Coconut Curry Lentils

Yield: 4 servings | Prep time: 10 minutes | Cook time: 1 hour

Ingredients:

- 1 cup dry brown lentils, rinsed
- 1 can (14 oz / 400ml) coconut milk
- 1 onion, diced
- 2 cloves garlic, minced
- 1 tablespoon curry powder
- 1 teaspoon ground turmeric
- 1 teaspoon ground cumin
- 1/2 teaspoon ground coriander
- Salt and pepper to taste
- Fresh cilantro, chopped, for garnish

Directions:

1. Preheat the sous vide water bath to 185°F (85°C).
2. In a large vacuum-sealable bag, combine the dry brown lentils, diced onion, minced garlic, coconut milk, curry powder, ground turmeric, ground cumin, ground coriander, salt, and pepper.
3. Seal the bag using a vacuum sealer, ensuring all the air is removed.
4. Once the water bath is ready, submerge the bag in the water bath and cook for 1 hour.
5. After 1 hour, carefully remove the bag from the water bath and open it.
6. Stir the lentil mixture well, ensuring all ingredients are evenly combined.
7. Serve the coconut curry lentils hot, garnished with chopped fresh cilantro.

Nutritional information: Approximately 300 calories, 12g protein, 30g carbohydrates, 15g fat, 8g fiber, 0mg cholesterol, 300mg sodium, 600mg potassium.

Chapter 9 Desserts

Sous Vide Crème Brûlée

Yield: 4 servings | Prep time: 10 minutes | Cook time: 1 hour and 30 minutes

Ingredients:

- 4 large egg yolks
- 1/4 cup (50g) granulated sugar
- 1 teaspoon vanilla extract
- 1 cup (240ml) heavy cream
- 1/2 cup (120ml) whole milk
- Pinch of salt
- 2 tablespoons (25g) granulated sugar (for caramelizing)

Directions:

1. Preheat the sous vide water bath to 176°F (80°C).
2. In a bowl, whisk together the egg yolks, 1/4 cup of sugar, and vanilla extract until well combined.
3. In a saucepan, heat the heavy cream, whole milk, and a pinch of salt over medium heat until it just starts to simmer. Remove from heat.
4. Slowly pour the hot cream mixture into the bowl with the egg yolk mixture, whisking constantly to combine.
5. Strain the mixture through a fine-mesh sieve to remove any lumps.
6. Divide the mixture evenly among ramekins or jars.
7. Seal each ramekin or jar with a lid or with plastic wrap.
8. Once the water bath is ready, submerge the ramekins or jars in the water bath and cook for 1 hour and 30 minutes.
9. After cooking, carefully remove the ramekins or jars from the water bath and let them cool to room temperature.
10. Once cooled, refrigerate the crème brûlées for at least 4 hours or overnight to set.
11. Before serving, sprinkle a thin, even layer of granulated sugar on top of each crème brûlée. Use a kitchen torch to caramelize the sugar until it forms a golden brown crust.
12. Serve immediately and enjoy!

Nutritional information: Approximately 350 calories, 4g protein, 20g carbohydrates, 28g fat, 0g fiber, 340mg cholesterol, 50mg sodium, 100mg potassium.

Sous Vide Cheesecake

Yield: 4 servings | Prep time: 20 minutes | Cook time: 2 hours

Ingredients:

- 1 cup (200g) graham cracker crumbs
- 2 tablespoons (30g) granulated sugar
- 4 tablespoons (60g) unsalted butter, melted
- 16 oz (450g) cream cheese, softened
- 2/3 cup (130g) granulated sugar
- 2 large eggs
- 1/4 cup (60ml) sour cream
- 1 teaspoon vanilla extract

- Pinch of salt

Directions:

1. Preheat the sous vide water bath to 176°F (80°C).
2. In a bowl, mix the graham cracker crumbs, 2 tablespoons of sugar, and melted butter until well combined.
3. Press the crumb mixture into the bottom of a 7-inch springform pan to form the crust.
4. In another bowl, beat the cream cheese and 2/3 cup of sugar until smooth.
5. Add the eggs, one at a time, mixing well after each addition.
6. Stir in the sour cream, vanilla extract, and salt until combined.
7. Pour the cheesecake mixture over the crust in the springform pan and spread it evenly.
8. Cover the springform pan tightly with aluminum foil.
9. Place the springform pan in a large vacuum-sealable bag, ensuring the bag is sealed around the pan to prevent water from entering.
10. Once the water bath is ready, submerge the bag with the springform pan in the water bath and cook for 2 hours.
11. After 2 hours, carefully remove the springform pan from the water bath and let it cool to room temperature.
12. Refrigerate the cheesecake for at least 4 hours or overnight to set.
13. Once set, remove the cheesecake from the springform pan and slice.
14. Serve chilled and enjoy!

Nutritional information: Approximately 500 calories, 10g protein, 30g carbohydrates, 40g fat, 0g fiber, 220mg cholesterol, 300mg sodium, 200mg potassium.

Sous Vide Chocolate Lava Cake

Yield: 4 servings | Prep time: 15 minutes | Cook time: 1 hour
Ingredients:

- 4 ounces (113g) dark chocolate, chopped
- 1/2 cup (113g) unsalted butter
- 1/2 cup (100g) granulated sugar
- 2 large eggs
- 2 large egg yolks
- 1 teaspoon vanilla extract
- 1/4 cup (30g) all-purpose flour
- Pinch of salt
- Powdered sugar, for dusting
- Vanilla ice cream, for serving (optional)

Directions:

1. Preheat the sous vide water bath to 176°F (80°C).
2. In a microwave-safe bowl, melt the dark chocolate and unsalted butter together in the microwave in 30-second intervals, stirring between each interval until smooth. Let it cool slightly.
3. In a separate bowl, whisk together the granulated sugar, eggs, egg yolks, and vanilla extract until well combined.
4. Gradually whisk the melted chocolate mixture into the egg mixture until smooth.
5. Sift in the all-purpose flour and add a pinch of salt, then fold gently until just combined.
6. Divide the batter evenly among four 4-ounce ramekins.
7. Cover each ramekin tightly with aluminum foil.
8. Place the ramekins in a large vacuum-sealable bag, ensuring they are arranged in a single layer.
9. Seal the bag using a vacuum sealer, ensuring all the air is removed.

10. Once the water bath is ready, submerge the bag in the water bath and cook for 1 hour.
11. After 1 hour, carefully remove the ramekins from the water bath and let them cool for a few minutes.
12. Remove the aluminum foil from the ramekins and carefully invert each lava cake onto a plate.
13. Dust with powdered sugar and serve immediately, optionally with a scoop of vanilla ice cream.

Nutritional information: Approximately 450 calories, 7g protein, 30g carbohydrates, 35g fat, 3g fiber, 250mg cholesterol, 50mg sodium, 150mg potassium.

Sous Vide Poached Pears

Yield: 4 servings | Prep time: 10 minutes | Cook time: 2 hours
Ingredients:

- 4 ripe pears, peeled and cored
- 1 cup (240ml) red wine
- 1/2 cup (100g) granulated sugar
- 1 cinnamon stick
- 4 cloves
- 1 teaspoon vanilla extract
- Zest of 1 orange

Directions:

1. Preheat the sous vide water bath to 176°F (80°C).
2. In a small saucepan, combine the red wine, granulated sugar, cinnamon stick, cloves, vanilla extract, and orange zest. Bring to a simmer over medium heat and cook for 5 minutes, stirring occasionally, until the sugar is dissolved.
3. Place the peeled and cored pears in a vacuum-sealable bag.
4. Pour the red wine mixture over the pears in the bag.
5. Seal the bag using a vacuum sealer, ensuring all the air is removed.
6. Once the water bath is ready, submerge the bag in the water bath and cook for 2 hours.
7. After 2 hours, carefully remove the bag from the water bath and open it.
8. Remove the poached pears from the bag and transfer them to serving plates.
9. Optionally, strain the poaching liquid through a fine-mesh sieve and simmer it in a saucepan over medium heat until reduced and syrupy. Drizzle the syrup over the poached pears before serving.
10. Serve the sous vide poached pears warm or chilled, optionally with a scoop of vanilla ice cream or whipped cream.

Nutritional information: Approximately 200 calories, 1g protein, 40g carbohydrates, 0g fat, 5g fiber, 0mg cholesterol, 10mg sodium, 300mg potassium.

Sous Vide Bread Pudding

Yield: 4 servings | Prep time: 15 minutes | Cook time: 1 hour
Ingredients:

- 4 cups (about 200g) stale bread cubes (such as French or brioche)
- 2 cups (480ml) whole milk
- 3 large eggs
- 1/2 cup (100g) granulated sugar
- 1 teaspoon vanilla extract
- 1/2 teaspoon ground cinnamon

- Pinch of salt
- 1/2 cup (75g) raisins or chopped nuts (optional)
- Butter or cooking spray, for greasing

Directions:

1. Preheat the sous vide water bath to 176°F (80°C).
2. Grease a 7x7-inch baking dish with butter or cooking spray.
3. In a large bowl, whisk together the whole milk, eggs, granulated sugar, vanilla extract, ground cinnamon, and a pinch of salt until well combined.
4. Add the stale bread cubes to the bowl and gently toss until all the bread cubes are evenly coated with the milk mixture. Allow the bread to soak for about 10 minutes.
5. If using, fold in the raisins or chopped nuts into the bread mixture.
6. Transfer the bread mixture to the greased baking dish, spreading it out evenly.
7. Cover the baking dish tightly with aluminum foil.
8. Place the baking dish in a large vacuum-sealable bag, ensuring the bag is sealed around the dish to prevent water from entering.
9. Once the water bath is ready, submerge the bag with the baking dish in the water bath and cook for 1 hour.
10. After 1 hour, carefully remove the baking dish from the water bath and let it cool for a few minutes.
11. Remove the aluminum foil from the baking dish and serve the bread pudding warm, optionally topped with a dusting of powdered sugar or a dollop of whipped cream.

Nutritional information: Approximately 300 calories, 10g protein, 40g carbohydrates, 10g fat, 2g fiber, 150mg cholesterol, 200mg sodium, 250mg potassium.

Sous Vide Fruit Compote

Yield: 4 servings | Prep time: 10 minutes | Cook time: 1 hour

Ingredients:

- 2 cups mixed fresh or frozen fruits (such as berries, peaches, or apples), chopped if necessary
- 1/4 cup (50g) granulated sugar
- 1 tablespoon lemon juice
- 1 teaspoon vanilla extract
- Pinch of salt

Directions:

1. Preheat the sous vide water bath to 176°F (80°C).
2. In a vacuum-sealable bag, combine the mixed fruits, granulated sugar, lemon juice, vanilla extract, and a pinch of salt.
3. Seal the bag using a vacuum sealer, ensuring all the air is removed.
4. Once the water bath is ready, submerge the bag in the water bath and cook for 1 hour.
5. After 1 hour, carefully remove the bag from the water bath and let it cool slightly.
6. Open the bag and transfer the fruit compote to a serving bowl.
7. Serve the sous vide fruit compote warm or chilled, optionally with yogurt, ice cream, or whipped cream.

Nutritional information: Approximately 100 calories, 1g protein, 25g carbohydrates, 0g fat, 3g fiber, 0mg cholesterol, 5mg sodium, 150mg potassium.

Sous Vide Lemon Curd

Yield: 4 servings | Prep time: 10 minutes | Cook time: 1 hour

Ingredients:

- 3 large eggs
- 3/4 cup (150g) granulated sugar
- Zest of 2 lemons
- 1/2 cup (120ml) freshly squeezed lemon juice
- 1/2 cup (113g) unsalted butter, cubed

Directions:

1. Preheat the sous vide water bath to 167°F (75°C).
2. In a heatproof bowl, whisk together the eggs, granulated sugar, and lemon zest until well combined.
3. Gradually whisk in the freshly squeezed lemon juice until smooth.
4. Place the bowl over a pot of simmering water (double boiler) and cook, stirring constantly, until the mixture thickens enough to coat the back of a spoon, about 8-10 minutes.
5. Remove the bowl from the heat and gradually whisk in the cubed unsalted butter until melted and fully incorporated.
6. Strain the lemon curd through a fine-mesh sieve to remove any lumps or zest.
7. Transfer the strained lemon curd to a vacuum-sealable bag.
8. Seal the bag using a vacuum sealer, ensuring all the air is removed.
9. Once the water bath is ready, submerge the bag in the water bath and cook for 1 hour.
10. After 1 hour, carefully remove the bag from the water bath and let it cool to room temperature.
11. Refrigerate the lemon curd for at least 2 hours or until chilled and set.
12. Serve the sous vide lemon curd chilled and enjoy!

Nutritional information: Approximately 250 calories, 3g protein, 30g carbohydrates, 14g fat, 0g fiber, 185mg cholesterol, 10mg sodium, 100mg potassium.

Sous Vide Flan

Yield: 4 servings | Prep time: 15 minutes | Cook time: 1 hour

Ingredients:

- 4 large eggs
- 1 can (14 ounces) sweetened condensed milk
- 1 can (12 ounces) evaporated milk
- 1 teaspoon vanilla extract
- 1/2 cup (100g) granulated sugar, for caramelizing

Directions:

1. Preheat the sous vide water bath to 176°F (80°C).
2. In a mixing bowl, whisk together the eggs, sweetened condensed milk, evaporated milk, and vanilla extract until well combined.
3. Set aside while preparing the caramel.
4. In a small saucepan over medium heat, melt the granulated sugar, stirring constantly, until it turns golden brown and caramelizes. Be careful not to burn it.
5. Once the sugar has caramelized, quickly pour it into the bottoms of four 4-ounce ramekins, swirling each ramekin to evenly coat the bottom.
6. Allow the caramel to cool and harden in the ramekins.
7. Once the caramel has hardened, pour the flan mixture into each ramekin over the caramel.
8. Cover each ramekin tightly with aluminum foil.
9. Place the ramekins in a large vacuum-sealable bag, ensuring they are arranged in a single layer.

10. Seal the bag using a vacuum sealer, ensuring all the air is removed.
11. Once the water bath is ready, submerge the bag in the water bath and cook for 1 hour.
12. After 1 hour, carefully remove the ramekins from the water bath and let them cool to room temperature.
13. Once cooled, refrigerate the flan for at least 4 hours or overnight to set.
14. To serve, run a knife around the edge of each ramekin and invert the flan onto a plate, allowing the caramel to drizzle over the top.
15. Serve the sous vide flan chilled and enjoy!

Nutritional information: Approximately 300 calories, 9g protein, 40g carbohydrates, 12g fat, 0g fiber, 150mg cholesterol, 100mg sodium, 250mg potassium

Sous Vide Chocolate Mousse

Yield: 4 servings | Prep time: 10 minutes | Cook time: 1 hour
Ingredients:

- 7 ounces (200g) dark chocolate, chopped
- 1/2 cup (120ml) heavy cream
- 3 large eggs, separated
- 1/4 cup (50g) granulated sugar
- 1 teaspoon vanilla extract
- Pinch of salt

Directions:

1. Preheat the sous vide water bath to 160°F (71°C).
2. In a heatproof bowl, combine the chopped dark chocolate and heavy cream.
3. Place the bowl over a pot of simmering water (double boiler) and stir until the chocolate is melted and the mixture is smooth. Remove from heat and let it cool slightly.
4. In a separate bowl, whisk together the egg yolks, granulated sugar, vanilla extract, and a pinch of salt until well combined.
5. Slowly pour the melted chocolate mixture into the egg yolk mixture, whisking constantly, until smooth and well combined.
6. In another bowl, using a hand mixer or stand mixer, beat the egg whites until stiff peaks form.
7. Gently fold the beaten egg whites into the chocolate mixture until fully incorporated.
8. Divide the chocolate mousse mixture evenly among four 4-ounce ramekins or serving glasses.
9. Cover each ramekin tightly with aluminum foil.
10. Place the ramekins in a large vacuum-sealable bag, ensuring they are arranged in a single layer.
11. Seal the bag using a vacuum sealer, ensuring all the air is removed.
12. Once the water bath is ready, submerge the bag in the water bath and cook for 1 hour.
13. After 1 hour, carefully remove the ramekins from the water bath and let them cool to room temperature.
14. Refrigerate the chocolate mousse for at least 2 hours or until chilled and set.
15. Serve the sous vide chocolate mousse chilled, optionally topped with whipped cream and shaved chocolate.

Nutritional information: Approximately 300 calories, 5g protein, 25g carbohydrates, 20g fat, 3g fiber, 150mg cholesterol, 50mg sodium, 200mg potassium.

Sous Vide Tiramisu

Yield: 4 servings | Prep time: 30 minutes | Cook time: 2 hours
Ingredients:

- 2 large eggs, separated
- 1/2 cup (100g) granulated sugar, divided
- 8 ounces (225g) mascarpone cheese, softened
- 1/2 cup (120ml) heavy cream
- 1 teaspoon vanilla extract
- 1 cup (240ml) strong brewed coffee, cooled
- 2 tablespoons coffee liqueur (optional)
- 16 ladyfinger cookies
- Cocoa powder, for dusting

Directions:

1. Preheat the sous vide water bath to 176°F (80°C).
2. In a heatproof bowl, whisk together the egg yolks and 1/4 cup of granulated sugar until pale and creamy.
3. Add the mascarpone cheese to the egg yolk mixture and whisk until smooth and well combined.
4. In another bowl, beat the egg whites until soft peaks form. Gradually add the remaining 1/4 cup of granulated sugar and continue beating until stiff peaks form.
5. Gently fold the beaten egg whites into the mascarpone mixture until fully incorporated.
6. In a separate bowl, whip the heavy cream and vanilla extract until stiff peaks form. Fold the whipped cream into the mascarpone mixture until smooth.
7. In a shallow dish, combine the cooled brewed coffee and coffee liqueur (if using).
8. Dip each ladyfinger cookie into the coffee mixture briefly, ensuring they are soaked but not soggy.
9. Arrange a layer of soaked ladyfinger cookies in the bottom of each serving dish.
10. Spoon a layer of the mascarpone mixture over the soaked ladyfinger cookies.
11. Repeat the layers of soaked ladyfinger cookies and mascarpone mixture, finishing with a layer of mascarpone mixture on top.
12. Cover each serving dish tightly with plastic wrap.
13. Place the serving dishes in the sous vide water bath and cook for 2 hours.
14. After 2 hours, carefully remove the serving dishes from the water bath and let them cool to room temperature.
15. Once cooled, refrigerate the tiramisu for at least 4 hours or overnight to set.
16. Before serving, dust the top of each tiramisu with cocoa powder.
17. Serve the sous vide tiramisu chilled and enjoy!

Nutritional information: Approximately 400 calories, 7g protein, 30g carbohydrates, 28g fat, 1g fiber, 230mg cholesterol, 100mg sodium, 150mg potassium.

Conclusion

As we reach the end of this book, I hope you've discovered that gourmet cooking doesn't have to be intimidating. With the power of sous vide at your fingertips and the guidance of this cookbook, you've unlocked the secrets to preparing restaurant-quality meals easily and elegantly.

Cooking using sous vide technology is not a fashionable trend, as it might seem to the uninitiated observer. Rather, it is a natural need of the body of a modern person striving to live a full life. And first of all, to taste.

Dishes cooked in sous vide are distinguished by their delicate texture, rich taste, and aroma. Sous vide cooking preserves all the vitamins, proteins, and minerals. This is the benefit of dietary food with the taste of haute cuisine.

As you close the pages of this cookbook, remember that the adventure is just beginning. As you master each recipe and master each technique, you'll have the courage to explore new flavors, experiment with inventive combinations, and enjoy the endless possibilities that sous vide cooking has to offer.

Whether you're enjoying a quiet meal at home or sharing a feast with loved ones, let this book be your trusted companion in your culinary endeavors. Remember that the essence of cooking is not just the flavors that tantalize the taste buds, but also the joy of creativity and the memories shared around the table. Whether you're cooking for yourself or impressing guests, each dish, prepared with love and attention, becomes a masterpiece in itself. With creativity, a dash of passion, and a generous dose of Sous Vide magic, every dish is a masterpiece, and every meal is a reason to celebrate.

Thank you for trusting me with your culinary journey. May SOUS VIDE COOKBOOK: Effortless Recipes for Beginners continue to inspire and delight you as you embark on countless delicious adventures in the kitchen.

Happy cooking!

Made in the USA
Middletown, DE
04 September 2024